SONS
OF
LIBERTY

Recent Titles in
Contributions in American Studies
Series Editor: Robert H. Walker

SONS OF LIBERTY

The Masculine Mind in Nineteenth-Century America

DAVID G. PUGH

Contributions in American Studies, Number 68

GREENWOOD PRESS
WESTPORT, CONNECTICUT
LONDON, ENGLAND

Library of Congress Cataloging in Publication Data

Pugh, David G.
  Sons of liberty.

  (Contributions in American studies, ISSN 0084-9227 ;
no. 68)
  Bibliography: p.
  Includes index.
  1. Men—United States—Psychology. 2. Masculinity
(Psychology) 3. Men—United States—History—19th
century. 4. Men—United States—Political activity.
5. Women—United States—History—19th century.
6. National characteristics, American. I. Title.
II. Series.
HQ1090.3.P83   1983   305.3'1'0973   83-10755
ISBN 0-313-23934-7 (lib. bdg.)

Library of Congress Catalog Card Number: 83-10755
ISBN: 0-313-23934-7
ISSN: 0084-9227

First published in 1983

Greenwood Press
A division of Congressional Information Service, Inc.
88 Post Road West
Westport, Connecticut 06881

Printed in the United States of America

10 9 8 7 6 5 4 3 2 1

Copyright Acknowledgments

To Marcy

CONTENTS

PREFACE

Our age, it seems, bears witness to Emerson's observation in "The American Scholar" that Americans have a knack for becoming good fingers, necks, and stomachs but not whole and happy human beings. While I certainly have no magic formula for wholeness or happiness, one thing has become increasingly apparent to me over the years: a satisfying intellectual life involves, at some point, a movement toward integrated knowledge and synthesis, a putting together of pieces rather than a further dividing and subdividing of them. Certainly we need specialists—to argue otherwise would be silly and pointless, given the complexities of modern life and the knowledge we have thus far accumulated—but I would also suggest that specialization is, or should be, a means to an end and not an end in itself, whether in the sciences, the humanities, or the social sciences. In their approaches to discovery, thought, and learning, our best researchers, scholars, and teachers support this claim.

Similarly, Thoreau—known chiefly in humanities circles but no slouch as a scientist, either—wrote in a journal entry for May 6, 1854, that "the sum of what the writer of whatever class has to report is simply some human experience, whether he be poet or philosopher or man of science.... Senses that take cognizance of outward things merely are of no avail." He went on to lament that in studying the report of a scientific group, he found little life, only a batch of sterile, technical terms, and thus he suspected that "the life of these learned professors has been almost as inhuman and wooden as a rain-gauge or self-registering magnetic machine. They communicate no fact that rises to the temperature of blood-heat."

Indeed, one reason I felt drawn to cultural criticism initially was that it required neither a rejection of my academic specialty, American literature, nor the sociologist's deadpan reliance on quantification and a data base. Rather, it required a rethinking of literature and certain historical facts in what were, for me at any rate, new and invigorating ways. While the process, including the writing of this book, has often been freighted with frustration and a nagging sense of inadequacy in several areas, the results have been satisfying if only because I have been able to raise some questions that intrigue me and then attempt to answer them, or at least to speculate on them with what I hope will be considered intelligent and thought-provoking concepts.

Equally satisfying, if not more so, has been the fact that *Sons of Liberty* allowed me to work with various people who, each in his or her own way, represent the sort of integrated intellectual life mentioned above, and whatever merit this book may have reflects their efforts. In particular, I wish to thank Mary Land for the countless hours she invested in this project. Her expansive intellect and energetic critiques often stopped me cold but only so that I might reconsider my direction and, when necessary, reroute my thinking. Her willingness to share her own ideas and to examine mine, her example and her labor, will not be forgotten.

Likewise, I am indebted to Richard Law for his thoughtful suggestions—including some crucial ones regarding the structure of this book—as well as his sustained encouragement during the dark hours that always accompany the combined tasks of thinking and writing. His help, personal and professional, has shown a capacity for insight and sensitivity deserving not only my gratitude but my respect.

For their moral support and confidence in my work, I wish to thank John Elwood, LeRoy Ashby, Robert Frank, and David Robinson. Quiet men all, they have given of themselves without hesitation or fanfare, and any note of appreciation here is small recognition of their influence on me.

For his technical assistance and willingness to work under pressure of deadlines, my thanks to Geordie Duckler.

My wife, Marcia Pugh, not only proofread the entire manuscript twice, she helped me at every turn with her contagious energy and her rare humanity. Words can neither measure nor weigh her presence here, but it is pervasive nonetheless: a presence that has brought this work to completion and for which no substitute could ever have been found.

INTRODUCTION

Until quite recently, WASP males dominated the political, social, and economic affairs of this nation to such an extent that any effort to assess them historically *as men* could be dismissed as a superfluous analysis of the obvious. That is, men were men, and they were best suited to control and to lead by fiat: an exercise in circular logic intended for the preservation of the species. The notion that manliness is its own definition can be traced to the Jacksonian belief that direct action, rather than thoughtful consideration, was the best response to almost any situation and that men could be measured not by their deepest motivations, but by what they did based on those motivations. Yet Alexis de Tocqueville's *Democracy in America* probed beneath the rough-hewn exterior of the American male and found, among other things, a bristling ego, an entrepreneurial soul, and, perhaps most important, evidence of profound anxiety. These observations, coming as they did from an outsider with no personal stake in the passions of the time, were prophetic and suggested that manliness, or masculinity, must at some point be understood as a complex, psychosexual state of being. Thus, the great-deeds-of-great-men approach to history is as unsatisfactory as it is simplistic, and Tocqueville's study can be viewed as an important forerunner to the more sophisticated work of Sigmund Freud in human psychosexuality. Freud's contributions are, of course, legion, and his influence on this study—both direct and indirect via such cultural critics as Geoffrey Gorer, Leslie Fiedler, and Erik Erikson—is manifest. The focus here, therefore, is both psychological and historical in an effort to define and to understand a cultural phenomenon: the masculinity cult in American life.

While the cult took shape in the early decades of the nineteenth century and while men may have been men because they were up and doing, it was the tangled web of their maleness—rooted in anxiety and charged with sublimated energy—that made them who they were and what they were to become. The process had begun during the Revolution when, as Gorer and others have pointed out, the rebels, weary of being treated like unruly children with few of the rights of other Englishmen, achieved a victory which constituted a rejection of the Fatherland in general and the father-figure of King George III in particular.[1] The Sons of Liberty were thus freed to pursue their own destinies, and they promptly set about establishing a government that, through an ingenious system of checks and balances, would never be able to exercise the arbitrary, patriarchal authority under which Europeans labored. Freedom for these sons, at once exhilarating and frightening, meant that as individuals and as a nation, they were faced with the prospect of building a new life independent of the culture, the traditions, the class system, and the institutions of England. They were, in short, faced with growing up a long way from home.

Yet the rejection of the Fatherland did not ensure the kind of liberty Americans came to expect as the nation developed, and the awesome potential of the new land became apparent after the Louisiana Purchase in 1803. Rather, old resentments were stirred as men—sensing the boundless social, economic, and geographical opportunity in America—felt constrained by such European residues as restrictive voting laws, aristocratic privilege, limited access to public office, and authoritarian institutions such as the United States Bank, which seemed to repress rather than encourage unfettered competition. The oppressive Father had been defeated, and the restless sons projected their anxieties onto the only parent left—the Mother—and displaced them by seeing in their enemies such female qualities as smothering maternalism and effeminate inaction that could only lead to the degeneration of democracy and, therefore, the demise of the new democrat, the Jacksonian man. With the Revolution, America could never be considered masculine (i.e., a Fatherland) and as Gorer has shown with great clarity, Americans have always envisioned their nation and the land as feminine, which is to say, something to be revered by men but also something to be defeated and controlled by them as a means of expressing their maleness, their autonomy, by contrast. "America," Gorer claims, "in its benevolent, rich, idealistic aspects is envisaged (by Americans) as feminine; it is masculine only in its grasping and demanding aspects. The American land itself...is feminine; its possession has been on occasion wooing, on occasion seduction, and on occasion rape."[2]

In these terms, the dates 1828–1890 frame this study with the Age of Andrew Jackson and the Gilded Age, even though the rise of Jackson as a national hero actually began with his victory over the British at New Orleans in 1815 and the impact of the Gilded Age carried well into the twentieth century. Still, 1828 was the year Jackson broke the aristocratic hold on the presidency with his defeat of John Quincy Adams, and in the process Old Hickory became this nation's first official prototype of the manliness ethos. James Fenimore Cooper believed that the difference between Adams and Jackson was "altogether one of men" and that Jackson was preferable for such traits as his decisiveness and courage.[3] His actions spoke louder than polite words, and his apparent repudiation of stifling affectations concerning taste, education, and class symbolized America's overweening sense of rugged independence as did his fight against the Bank, an institution Jackson opposed—regardless of its restraints on inflation and wildcat speculation—simply because it had too much power. With these fundamental concepts in mind, the second chapter of this study will develop the idea that it was the Jacksonian mystique, not the real Jackson with ample power and aristocratic aspirations of his own, which expressed the sentiments of his time. These sentiments, as John Demos has noted, "called forth an appropriate character, which included strength, cunning, inventiveness, endurance—a whole range of traits henceforth defined as exclusively 'masculine.' "[4]

In 1890 the Bureau of the Census declared the frontier closed, and one of the major events in American history ended. Continental expansion and conquest coupled with industrialism and the triumphs of technology had provided nineteenth-century men their *raisons d'être*, their motivations and rationalizations for slaughtering the Indian, ravaging the land, and using the wilderness as a proving ground for WASP male supremacy. Inspired by the doctrine of Manifest Destiny and encouraged in the worship of progress by Herbert Spencer's social Darwinism, men vented their energies, their passions, and their resentments toward women in a frenetic attack on the virgin land. Mother Nature and her loyal children, the Indians, had to be controlled by men who were, in effect, new Adams in a new Eden, their hour come at last, and who gave to this mythological construct a peculiarly American twist, one sanctioned by the culture at large and based on the belief that the fittest, the toughest, the most ruthless would survive and prosper.

The frontier experience thus lodged itself in the American imagination where it remains to this day, and the nineteenth-century masculine manifesto—mythologized and ritualized—has continued to be a pervasive influence in American life. This ethos is especially noticeable in the realm of popular culture where deeply held values often receive exaggerated reinforcement: rodeos; western movies, television shows, and literature; such stylized rites of passage as the hunting trip; and the incessant, neurotic attempts of men to escape, however temporarily, female constraints and civilization. Today, as a century ago, men still seek to define their masculinity among other men and to vent the anxieties of another age toward women, heterosexuality, marriage, and anything that they believe to be effeminate and, therefore, a threat to manliness.

Not all men, of course, went west in the nineteenth century, and those who remained in the East found a frontier of another kind to conquer, the frontier of Wall Street and the marketplace. Tocqueville had observed this phenomenon during the age of Jackson when he noted that the man in the West was the same

as the man in the East and that both were essentially businessmen in search of the main chance. The difference was not one
of kind but one of unlimited change and growth—with an accompanying sense of both exhilaration and fear—while the latter
decades were distinguished by a penchant for order, constraint,
and control. Thus, for example, the Jacksonian policy of limited
government involvement in economic affairs was intended to
set men loose, but during the Gilded Age laissez-faire was used
by men to control huge portions of the economy and to limit
competition whenever possible. Or as John Higham has described it, the first half of the century was notable for "the swagger that accompanied it—the soaring, inflated, even boundless
character of its affirmations" while the second half saw a shift
"from diffusion to concentration, from spontaneity to order."[5]

With the end of the Civil War, the two fronts of the frontier
had been established, and the men of post-bellum America
showed how well they had learned the lessons of their Jacksonian fathers. The cult of the self-made man and the philosophy
of laissez-faire gave them the license they needed and, social
Darwinists to the core, they confiscated huge chunks of land,
built great machines and factories, fixed prices via secret alliances, and formed their empires with oil, coal, and steel. Thus,
the prophets of profit and progress—Rockefeller, Carnegie, Vanderbilt, Morgan, Gould, et al.—became the cultural heroes for
their time just as Jackson had been for his, and these new symbols of the manliness ethos represented the ideological and psychological shifts that had occurred between the time of Jackson
and the age of enterprise that followed after the war. Now change
and reform were to be feared, order and harmony to be secured
at any price, and this mood of retrenchment was intensified by
the growing presence of immigrants and emancipated blacks
who threatened traditional WASP superiority and power.

A historical assessment of masculinity must, however, do more
than study male behavior and men's thoughts concerning their
manliness since they did not live in a cultural vacuum, however
often they may have tried. In other words, because the nature
of masculinity is psychosexual and because men cultivated manliness as a means of distinguishing themselves from the "weaker
sex," their attitudes toward women and sexuality are crucial to

an understanding of the masculinity cult. The central chapter of
this work is thus devoted to an analysis of the role women played
in nineteenth-century American life. It is not a study of women
and female roles *per se* but an effort to comprehend nineteenth-
century manliness by examining how women were perceived
from the male point of view and how they reacted because of
it.

Women were, after all, a part of the culture, too, and while
they may have been shielded or even barred from certain activities considered to be in the male domain, they were often keenly
aware of the cultural attitudes defining them as women and the
pressures men claimed were (or should be) theirs alone to bear.
Indeed, many women were able to accommodate masculine ideology and at the same time circumvent it—e.g., Catharine
Beecher, Sarah Hale, and their followers—and the notion that
all women were passive victims whose situation has been righted
only during the feminist movement of the past twenty or so
years must be challenged by a more balanced assessment. Certainly women were relegated by men to hearth, home, and the
nonsexual role of motherhood to neutralize them as threats to
male autonomy and as competitors in the manly world beyond
the front porch, but they were also a vital force in the culture
and contributed a great deal to education, the arts, social progress, and cultural harmony, not to mention the abolitionist
movement and early political reform leading to eventual enfranchisement. The chapter titled "The Female Foil" is not concerned with arguing for the historical importance of these and
other phenomena concerning women—that much is accepted as
obvious—but with how and why men reacted and thought the
way they did when confronted with what was popularly called
"the woman question." Male responses to that "question" revealed a snarled web of anxiety, sexual repression and sublimation, and, perhaps most interesting of all, an unconscious,
paradoxical belief that manliness could best be attained through
sexual autonomy from women.

Given these and other related perspectives on the masculinity
cult, it might be said that such an approach, or variety of approaches, is hopelessly muddled. Yet it is precisely this method
of investigation—cross-cultural and unrestrained by traditional

divisions of academic labor—that enhances an integrated understanding of a complex phenomenon, one that has helped to shape modern American life. History, after all, is not something "back there" but a process of becoming, a process involving not only people's actions and thoughts but the emotional, cultural, mythological, and psychosexual forces that have motivated them. Elizabeth Fox-Genovese has stated that "among psychohistory's heaviest crosses, it bears that of the goal of clinical precision. In point of fact, no psychohistorian...is a practicing analyst; the subjects of psychohistorical analysis, being dead, speak only indirectly through writing, song, story, etc.; they cannot free-associate, nor can they be cured."[6] Yet whether or not various historical figures and personalities could have used some curing, they need to be understood in more than the strictly historical sense of time, place, and action. This study is, therefore, as much a search for a historical perspective as for history itself, and it attempts to synthesize a wide range of cultural criticism: e.g., Thorstein Veblen's cultural economics, Stanley Diamond's analysis of tribalism and his plea for new models of the primitive, Erik H. Erikson's speculations on the American identity and "Mom," and Leslie Fiedler's assessment of literature based in part on the battle of the sexes and the threat of annihilation men saw in any genuine commitment to heterosexual love.

Fusing several angles of vision to form still another in no way suggests an attempt at a final, definitive interpretation of a historical trend, and the nature of this work remains, in many ways, speculative. American life, like any other well-developed culture, is a complex matter, and the cultural critic's efforts to explain it are often as difficult as his subject. Addressing this problem in *Childhood and Society*, Erik Erikson sees the cultural critic in the precarious position of trying to achieve some distance or detachment from his subject without denying the validity of his own impressions and judgments drawn from many years of cultural osmosis. Ultimately, he claims, the only healthy way for an American to write about America is to set forth an argument and overstate it.[7] Still, the danger remains that accuracy will be lost in overstatement, and it is hoped that trap has been avoided here, along with others such as unqualified dullness and historical nit-picking.

There is no desire here to point an accusatory finger at nine-teenth-century males, to indict them in any way, but rather to understand them and the nature of the power they sought. This is the way in which the cultural critic tries to order—or at least to comprehend—the chaos of American experience. Once the smoke of the Revolution had cleared, that chaos began in the first decades of the nineteenth century, and according to Bertram Wyatt-Brown, it was an age of self-conscious, "passionate chest-thumping" because "in times of rapid social, industrial, and political expansion, men sometimes find it necessary to portray themselves in such elemental terms."[8] And that, in a nutshell, describes how and why men expressed their masculinity, the manliness ethos, in the ways that they did and often still do today.

SONS
OF
LIBERTY

1

THE JACKSONIAN MYSTIQUE

The rise of Andrew Jackson to president of the United States was the result of both a widespread movement and a relatively sophisticated propaganda campaign conducted by Jacksonian political spokesmen who defined political issues in a conscious attempt to appeal to the early nineteenth-century popular imagination. As Marvin Meyers describes them, these issues were defined by Jacksonian politicians as "equality against privilege, liberty against domination, honest work against idle exploit; natural dignity against factitious superiority; patriotic conservatism against alien innovation; progress against dead precedent. A first ungraded inventory shows only a troubled mind groping for names to fit its discontent."[1] This "troubled" mind, which Meyers describes and whose anxieties were projected onto the political and economic issues of the day, reveals an underlying but distinctly masculine point of view just beginning to emerge in American life. Indeed, the roots of a masculinity cult in America lay in the anxious efforts of men in the Age of Jackson to define their social, political, and economic positions within a nation attempting to do the same things in the broader community of nations. Thus, one of the main reasons for the popularity of the

Jacksonian movement was the fact that it allied itself with the anxieties of the time and focused its energy in struggles—moral as well as political—against various presumed enemies such as the United States Bank, the upper classes, and new centers of power in government: in other words, tangible scapegoats.

CULTURAL FERMENT AND AN AGE OF ANXIETY

Jacksonian America was, in the words of John Higham, "a culture with a very indistinct sense of limits, a culture characterized by a spirit of boundlessness," and it comprised fluidity and adaptability on the one hand, a dangerous lack of cohesion on the other.[2] Horizontal and vertical mobility was suddenly a reality; old institutions and customs of deference were eroding; the family was changing from a tightly bound, extended unit to a nuclear one; economics had outgrown the simple barter system to become more complex; and by the 1840s disparate ethnic groups were facing off as Irish Catholics swarmed to America: all of which indicate the culture shock of massive, unassimilable change that left men disoriented, without the security of traditional class boundaries, and filled with both awe and fear over the new egalitarianism. Like the ocean and the land stretching endlessly before the self-reliant man, equality and opportunity seemed to confirm the transcendentalists' belief in infinite possibilities and, somewhat later, Whitman's celebration of the Open Road; yet they also produced a sense of fluidity, of formlessness, that could only inspire uneasiness and the free-floating anxiety of the displaced person with nowhere to go but everywhere.

The famous New England preacher William Ellery Channing helped to define the age of Jackson as an age of anxiety when, in 1841, he observed that "in looking at our age I am struck immediately with one commanding characteristic, and that is the tendency in all its movements to expansion, to diffusion, to universality.... This tendency is directly opposed to the spirit of exclusiveness, restriction, narrowness, monopoly, which has prevailed in past ages.... Undoubtedly this is a perilous tendency. Men forget the limits of their powers. They question the infinite, the unsearchable, with an audacious self-reliance."[3] And it was Channing and men like him—conservative, New England traditionalists—who were swept aside by the enthusiasms of the age, by a rush of activity demanding men of action rather than staid commentators and resulting in the victory of Andrew Jackson over John Quincy Adams in 1828. The age needed a Jackson, a mythologized military hero whose aggressiveness matched a period in America's history when the country resembled, in the words of one observer, "a bivouac rather than a nation, a grand army moving from the Atlantic to the Pacific, and pitching tents along the way."[4] Moreover, with a second victory over England in 1815, Americans were possessed by a fighting spirit, and the times were filled with evangelical and secular crusades revealing anxious men at once concerned with energetically pursuing their newly confirmed freedom and protecting themselves, often violently, from a culture in danger of spinning out of control. Thus, it was not mere historical coincidence that the age that needed and in fact created Jackson, also fought against aristocratic privilege and the "Monster Bank," while rioting against Catholics, Mormons, blacks, and abolitionists and denouncing the early leaders of the feminist movement.

Concerning this cultural ferment, Higham has pointed out that "the first half of the nineteenth century has had no monopoly on violence in American history. But what distinguished the tumult of the period from earlier ones was the swagger that accompanied it—the soaring, inflated, even boundless character of its affirmations."[5] Or as Bertram Wyatt-Brown has put it, "passionate chest-thumping was highly self-conscious in these decades. . . . The age required assertions of warrior-spirit and 'forthright' denunciations of an adversary's 'cowardice and servility' from its young men. It is always hard to be reasonable and conciliatory when claims and counter-claims of masculinity and degeneracy become common in public exchange. In times of rapid social, industrial, and political expansion, men sometimes find it necessary to portray themselves in such elemental terms."[6] The age was one of great hopes and great fears—shifting anxieties—in which evangelists exhorted men to be saved from themselves and other equally passionate crusaders fought to save men from each other: the anti-abolitionist, for example, feared racial degeneration; the abolitionist saw slavery as the ultimate cultural sanction of moral depravity; and the ruling power type, the White Anglo-Saxon Protestant, chafed at the influx of papist foreigners with their dangerous doctrines, strange customs, and economic aspirations. Self-righteousness, no less than self-reliance, was a mark of the times and far from shedding all inhibitions, "nineteenth-century Americans ordinarily sought release only from the material and institutional confinements that bound them to a fixed place or a given social role. In proportion as those external ties relaxed, the internalized restraints of conscience and of public opinion tightened. Thus the Age of Boundlessness combined a passion for freedom with an exceptionally strict moral code."[7] Men tried to define themselves in a tension-filled milieu in which contrary forces of expansiveness and constriction, of amoral development of self and moral responsibility to others, tugged at them.

American men often sought self-definition not through direct confrontation with society but by first evading society and then reuniting with it—flight and return, boundlessness and consolidation—and thereby enacting one of the most dominant patterns in our culture as set forth by Washington Irving's "Rip Van Winkle" in 1819. Because the story is set in both pre- and post-revolutionary America, it provided a metaphor of the times in which it was actually written because Rip is the first example in our native literature of the profound psychological effects that particular war was to have on nineteenth-century men. That is, when Rip picked up his musket, called his dog Wolf to his side, and left his shrewish wife, their home, and the village for the peaceful woods, he established an archetypal American character responding to society and domestic life in the only way he knew how: flight to avoid persecution. To understand the implications of this event for future generations of American men will, however, require a psychological framework in which to place it.

In *The American People*, Geoffrey Gorer recalls Freud's *Totem and Taboo* and its mythological account of the origins of civilization. The sons of a tyrannical father conspire to murder him but, once the deed has been accomplished, they are overwhelmed by what they have done and fearful that one of their kind might replace the dead oppressor. To ensure their security against this internal threat, the newly liberated sons devise an agreement establishing their legal equality and repudiating the power and privileges formerly enjoyed by the father. Gorer compares this Freudian construct with the American experience during the Revolution. "England," he points out, "the England of George III and Lord North, takes the place of the despotic and tyrannical father, the American colonists that of the conspiring sons, and the Declaration of Independence and the American Constitution that of the compact by which all Americans are guaranteed freedom and equality on the basis of the common renunciation of all authority over people, which had been the father's most hated and most envied privilege."[8] While this comparison relies on an analogy between a historical event and a parable, it nonetheless reveals a couple of important themes regarding the American character as it took form in the nineteenth century. First, what Gorer calls "emotional egalitarianism" declares that all white American men should have equal opportunity and legal rights; second, authority should be resisted, and those who either hold it or seek it should be regarded as "potential enemies and usurpers."[9]

Yet the Sons of Liberty and their sons to follow—the descendents of Rip Van Winkle, so to speak—found that authority had not been ousted by the Revolution and the rejection of the tyrannical father. Thus, if men were to mature, to develop, as individuals and as a nation, authority had to be rejected once again, this time in the form of the only parent left: the female, wife and mother. Rip's mistake was that he had attempted to purge his anxieties with an actual rejection, or avoidance, of the female authority in his life, and he was, therefore, not only morally derelict in his duty to her but doomed to remain forever a boy because he awoke to find that he had neither a father- nor a mother-figure, the one having been rejected by his countrymen while he slept, the other having died.

Nineteenth-century men, on the other hand, did not attempt such a direct route to psychological freedom, and the only figure of authority left to them—the mother—became both a necessary moral force and a source of contempt. That contempt was not expressed directly, however, but vented through a more subtle and complex process, so that the anxieties men felt in a culture suddenly set loose and beset with turmoil were indirectly pro-

jected onto women and displaced by seeing various enemies as
a smothering maternal figure (i.e., the Bank) or as effeminate
snobs (i.e., aristocrats). Yet this process only created further
psychological tension since the American male, fatherless by
choice, carried within him the female voice of restraint and civilization, a point Gorer makes in discussing how the male child,
raised primarily by the mother, comes to possess many more of
her values than the father's, a process referred to as "the idiosyncratic feature of the American conscience."[10] As Gorer explains, because Duty and Right Conduct are feminine figures,
the role of the daughter is relatively easy and explicit, but for
the American son, the situation is far more complicated and
confusing:

> He carries around, as it were encapsulated inside him, an ethical,
> admonitory, censorious mother. In all the spheres where moral
> considerations are meant to operate...men act as though they
> were being guided by (or rebelling against) rules and prohibitions
> enunciated by a moral mother. For the mother—actual or inter-
> nalized—not only gives her sons rules for proper behavior in the
> spheres in which she and her kind play a role; she also sets rules
> of behavior in spheres to which she and her sex have no en-
> try.... The fact that the rules for moral conduct are felt to emanate
> from a feminine source is a source of considerable confusion to
> American men. They tend to resent such interference with their
> own behavior, and yet are unable to ignore it, since the insistent
> maternal conscience is a part of their personality.... A second
> result of this state of affairs is that all the niceties of masculine
> behavior—modesty, politeness, neatness, cleanliness—come to be
> regarded as concessions to feminine demands, and not good in
> themselves as part of the behavior of a proper man. As such they
> become irksome and are sloughed off—with relief but not without
> guilt—whenever a suitable occasion presents itself.[11]

In other words, men both needed their women and sought
to avoid them; they both praised women directly and saw indirectly in their enemies those female qualities that a masculine
sensibility could not endure. Certainly Rip heard the voice of
an admonitory mother but because he ignored it and then took
an escape route lasting too long, he was first an irresponsible

child and then a psychological orphan. Nineteenth-century men incorporated the Rip Van Winkle prototype with some variations intended to avoid a permanent state of arrested adolescence, and thus they often fled—in spirit if not in fact—what they felt were female constraints long enough to discover a sense of manly independence from them. They returned soon enough, however, haunted either by the guilt of having evaded moral responsibility or by the fears uncovered along the way. Leslie Fiedler has commented on "Rip Van Winkle" that "ever since, the typical male protagonist of our fiction has been a man on the run, harried into the forest and out to sea, down the river or into combat—anywhere to avoid 'civilization,' which is to say, the confrontation of a man and woman which leads to the fall to sex, marriage, and responsibility."[12] And once the father's constraining force had been rejected by the Revolution, Irving's tale assumed added significance for the time in which it was written as Rip, feeling badgered and forlorn for what amounts to his own neglect of duty in a civilized society, projects his anxiety onto the wife-mother figure: Europe's replacement in the nineteenth-century male mind. The fact that Rip did this prior to the Revolution made no difference to that mind (or its twentieth-century equivalent) because for it, the rejection of the father had been completed and reinforced by the War of 1812. Throughout the years, Americans have thus been naturally predisposed to view "Rip Van Winkle" in those psychological terms that are truly American, and the story has imbedded itself in America's collective consciousness, for readers and nonreaders alike. And it was for early nineteenth-century men that the character of Rip Van Winkle had its first important implications because they found themselves in a pressurized culture that placed a premium on the male's growing up, making something of himself, and leaving childhood dependence behind. In this regard, Philip Young's psychological study of Rip suggests that

> he was not an adult, but a child playing with children, a kid with a dog. He lived with his wife, to be sure, but only in a manner of speaking, for he accepted instead his "only alternative": "to take gun in hand and stroll away into the woods." . . . At the inn with the menfolk, Rip shows that he wants to be a father. But at

home he is a son, and not up to it: he is the son who wants to be the father, but his mother won't let him. He represents, to be technical for a moment, the ego arrested at the infantile level in an Oedipal situation; under pressure he reverts all the way back to the sleep of the womb.[13]

Once in the woods, at sea, or on a raft enshrouded in fog, however, our literary males do not discover the freedom they have longed for but terror, threats of annihilation, or, in Rip Van Winkle's case, profound anxiety as he joins the all-male gathering in the mountains and expects to find the same fellowship he had enjoyed among "a kind of perpetual club of the sages, philosophers, and other idle personages of the village."[14] Rip, for whom life had grown "worse and worse...as years of matrimony rolled on," finds in the woods a dour group of sportsmen who "stared at him with such fixed, statue-like gaze, and such strange, uncouth, lack-lustre countenances, that his heart turned within him, and his knees smote together. His companion now emptied the contents of the keg into large flagons, and made signs to him to wait upon the company. He obeyed with fear and trembling; they quaffed the liquor in profound silence, and then returned to their game" (pp. 94, 98). Rip moves from civilization to nature and back again, and he has, in the process, become an exaggerated psychological model—a telling caricature—of the restless American male:

> Rip is a stereotype of the American male as seen from abroad, or in some jaundiced quarters at home: he is perfectly the jolly overgrown child, abysmally ignorant of his own wife and the whole world of adult men—perpetually "one of the boys," hanging around what they are pleased to think of as a "perpetual men's club"; a disguised Rotarian who simply will not and cannot grow up. In moments of candor we will probably admit that a stereotype with no germ of truth in it could not exist: some such mythic America, some such mythic American, exist both actually and in the consciousness of the world. Rip will do very well as their prototype.[15]

Ever since Rip Van Winkle's legendary flight from female civilization and his eventual return to it, America's fictional, metaphorical heroes have moved between two worlds—domestic and wild—both of which are unsavory and compel men to seek the collective security of other males, to be admitted as one of the gang only to be betrayed by them as well in the end. This wanderer, as Fiedler points out,

> feels himself without protection, more motherless child than free man. To be sure, there is a substitute for wife or mother presumably waiting in the green heart of nature; the natural man, the good companion, pagan and unashamed—Queequeg or Chingachgook or Nigger Jim. But the figure of the natural man is ambiguous, a dream and a nightmare at once. The other face of Chingachgook is Injun Joe, the killer in the graveyard and the haunter of caves; Nigger Jim is also the Babo of Melville's "Benito Cereno," the humble servant whose name means "papa" holding the razor to his master's throat; and finally the dark-skinned companion becomes the "Black Man," which is a traditional American name for the Devil himself.[16]

Behind the appearance of humor and high adventure in America's best literature (as in the culture) lurk guilt and fear, guilt over the hero's flight itself and fear of the bizarre dangers along the way, or in Fiedler's terms, "our literature as a whole at times seems a chamber of horrors disguised as an amusement park 'fun house,' where we pay to play at terror and are confronted in the innermost chamber with a series of interreflecting mirrors which present us with a thousand versions of our own face."[17]

Like such literary and folk heroes as Natty Bumppo, Rip Van Winkle, and Daniel Boone, man in the nineteenth century tried to lose himself in nature in order to find himself. In the process, he gave form to an archetypal, unconscious attitude toward nature—love and hate—as old as Adam's in the Garden of Eden, as noticeable as the Puritan's in the New World, and as recent as Bumppo's in a forest both pantheistically sublime and hostile. The undefiled West was a refuge for threatened men, but it was also, and more importantly, an adversary to be conquered, a resource to be plundered and plowed. They were Ahabs exerting themselves over other men and facing, with pathological irony, the possibility of their own destruction. This view of men as restless and anxious is set forth by Marvin Meyers:

The men of the middle, preponderant in democratic times and overwhelmingly so in America, are unquiet souls, whipped into motion by acquisitive hunger and then arrested by possessive fears. When Tocqueville portrays such men as the "natural enemies of violent commotions," he has in mind no inert lump of a dozing bourgeois but a nervous striver whose apprehensions mount with his success. The democratic competitor, shifting his efforts fluidly toward the quick opening to relative economic success (as the key to all felicity), finds himself in the midst of a universal competition of equals. With all the parts of his universe, himself included, in erratic motion, with no fixed terminus and no secure resting place, the democrat develops an acute awareness of loss and failure. He is never the contented success; rarely the jealous miser; and typically the unrelenting acquisitor, casting a nervous backward glance at what he has already gained.[18]

It was in this culture, a nation of men "in erratic motion, with no fixed terminus and no secure resting place," that the Jacksonian mystique naturally took hold to make Andrew Jackson the perfect model of the manliness ethos, the inevitable response to the turbulence of the times.

If any single trait characterized the struggling American male in the first half of the nineteenth century, it was a certain restlessness, a free-floating anxiety, in the conduct of his affairs that, paradoxically, caused him to fight for economic progress as a way of asserting his individuality even as he ached for such old republican archetypes as the yeoman farmer who, content with the status quo, lived a peaceful, subsistence life. The belief in such myths as this one reveals the perennial American nostalgia for "the good old days," a wistful ignoring of the fact that subsistence farming was grueling, grubby, often futile work. Yet the myth persisted against the culture's developing infatuation with personal progress and profit, and such divided loyalty helped to separate the Jacksonians from the Whigs because the latter, while espousing the virtues of old republican ways, really only used the past as a sentimental device to justify their belief in progress through tariffs and banks. "Webster wept in memory of his father's forest hut; zealous clerks helped to clutter city streets with Harrison log cabins—but they [Whigs] felt no serious tension between past and present. Their cabin was a nostalgic prop, a publicity gimmick without focused moral content."[19] In their belief that Whigs felt no moral qualms about slighting the common man's role in the nation's brief but remarkable history, the Jacksonians reasserted the Enlightenment credo by seeing the privileged class as the enemy and sought to retain the character traits of the eighteenth-century yeoman by applying them in a new context: mobility rather than the sedentary life, personal betterment rather than mere subsistence. "Opportunity" was the byword of the time, and the Jacksonians felt its importance because they had found and promoted in their namesake a symbolic example of how far opportunity could be taken by the man ready to act in a rapidly changing world.

THE JACKSONIAN RESPONSE

Andrew Jackson, the nation's first nonaristocratic president, was the paradigm of the rugged individual for those who believed in him, and he made absolute moral judgments against such evils as the Bank since he saw it as the major impediment to retrieving old republican, Jeffersonian values. He advocated action rather than intellectual assessment, response based on a clear notion of right over wrong, so that "his presidential messages are ragged political philosophy, tendentious accounting, crude policy. Political opponents mocked the contents, but ruefully acknowledged the impressive popular effect. Jackson offered a broad public a moral definition of their situation, a definition that seemed to strike home."[20] The rise of egalitarian politics also drew the battle line between the common man and the aristocrat, between planters, farmers, mechanics, and laborers whom Jackson called in a typically masculine metaphor "the bone and sinew of the country" whose success "depends upon their own industry and economy" and those who relied on inherited wealth and prestige.[21] Richard Hofstadter has noted that "as the demand for the rights of the common man took form in nineteenth-century America, it included a program for free elementary education, but it also carried with it a dark and sullen suspicion of high culture, as a creation of the enemy."[22] In the Bank as an evil institution and the wealthy as an immoral class, Jackson and his followers discovered the necessary friction to propel Old Hickory into the White House, a push to power that defied and broke established lines of ascendancy to the presidency and one calculated to gain popular support as much through myth and lore about Jackson as fact.

It was the mystique surrounding Jackson that made him a national hero, what John William Ward has called "A Symbol for an Age," and it was here, in the realm of popular image, that Jackson became the prototype of the American male. Oddly enough, James Fenimore Cooper, who could never resolve his own ambivalence over aristocracy versus democracy, helped to build the Jacksonian prototype with his descriptions of Old Hickory. In *Notions of the Americans*, Cooper claims that the distinction to be made between Jackson and Adams in 1828 was one of manliness, and Jackson was the better of the two for such traits as decisiveness, courage, and tough-minded independence.[23] And in *Home as Found*, the Commodore declares that Old Hickory is a true man because he is "tough, sir; tough as a day in February on this lake. All fins, and gills, and bones," a description of Jackson reminiscent of his own words about the common man being "the bone and sinew of the country."[24] Cooper's characterization of Jackson is given through an old man living on the last remnants of old republican, conservative values, a man who was either unaware of, or chose to ignore, Adams's own tenacity as a political leader which would culminate in his death on the floor of the House of Representatives after a seventy-two-hour speech on behalf of opponents of slavery. For the Commodore and many of his countrymen, Jackson personified what they admired most in themselves, a point one of his eulogizers was proud to make: "He was the imbodiment [*sic*] of the true spirit of the nation in which he lived. . . . And why? because they see in him their own image. Because, in him is concentrated the spirit that has burned in their own bosom. . . . Because his countrymen saw their image and spirit in Andrew Jackson, they bestowed their honor and admiration upon him."[25]

A nation trying to define itself geographically while changing politically and growing economically needed a new kind of hero to lead it, someone of the land itself who had been tested for toughness and whose elevation to the status of hero depended on something more than birthright. Andrew Jackson was that man and, like most cultural heroes, his popular image was determined by what the people needed. Emerging, therefore, rough-hewn from the woods of Tennessee rather than polished by the aristocratic traditions of the South or New England, Jackson exhibited uncultured tastes and an untutored mind for public view, traits well suited to a time of raw, often violent energy. He further proved himself, as so many national heroes and presidents have, with his military exploits, most notably his famous defeat of the British at the Battle of New Orleans in 1815. A significant event for other than strictly military or political reasons, it confirmed America's earlier rejection of the Fatherland, which Jackson and other men his age could remember as a momentous part of their boyhood.

The ascent of Andrew Jackson to national hero and President of the United States further expressed this rejection of Old World civilization—a major theme of Cooper's leatherstocking novels—and extended the idealized character of Natty Bumppo beyond Cooper's vision to define a major anxiety of the age. That is, the rural American, believing as he did in the value of individualism and the simple, rustic life, was nonetheless a part of a dynamic culture and a fledgling member of the cult of progress; and common men, especially those who saw themselves as men of nature, were always casting nervous glances over their shoulders at the East behind them as they continued to move to the West in search of both the individualism they craved and the riches they could not resist as a means of gaining that individualism.

While the frontier stood fairly close to the Atlantic seaboard and major American cities were only beginning to become commercial and cultural centers of power, rural democrats still looked beyond the East to Europe as the object of their contempt. Later, during the decades after 1815, an urbanized, industrialized, sophisticated East—now an epicene figure in the mind of the fatherless American male—would replace Europe as the primary target of scorn, and the western descendants of the mythical Kentucky riflemen who fought with Jackson (the midwest farmer, the cowboy, the mountain man) would express their distrust of the elitism and corruption of the East by leaving it. According to Richard Slotkin, "the western view of the East...was much like the eastern view of Europe. The East was the area of civilization, the home country from which westerners had emigrated and whose ways they had rejected in favor of those the wilderness had impelled them to adopt. New York was the Nineveh to which western evangelists like Charles G. Finney came, preaching against the intellectual Pharisees."[26]

Fearing civilization, its class system, social conformity, and moral obligations and constraints, Americans made the West—with its limitless space and undefiled nature—a grand symbol of freedom, a refuge for an endangered species who felt they had earned their independence with the Revolution but who still felt threatened by eastern influence and authority in the nineteenth century. Thus, like Natty Bumppo and Daniel Boone, they fled further into the forest, nature, and the West, escaping as best they could the anonymity and domestication civilization implied. Eventually, of course, the westward movement would end at the shores of the Pacific Ocean and, ironically, with nowhere else to go, men began to build and civilize until, financed by eastern speculators, they had transformed the West Coast into a second East complete with cities functioning as centers of trade and aspiring to the sophistication and culture of their eastern forerunners. Thus, by 1890 when the Bureau of Census officially declared the frontier closed, the so-called rugged individual found himself trapped between two barriers, one geographical, the other psychological, and his flight had come full circle, even though he believed he had been traveling in a straight line.

In his discussion of the mythological Daniel Boone and the frontiersman in *Virgin Land*, Henry Nash Smith tells of Edwin James who, during a visit to Fort Osage in 1819, heard about Boone's claim that it was time to move further west "when he could no longer fell a tree for fuel so that its top would lie within a few yards of the door of his cabin," and this prompted James to observe that the peculiar behavior of frontiersmen demonstrated "a manifest propensity, particularly in the males, to remove westward, for which it is not easy to account."[27] According to James, it was the West that offered a life "wherein the artificial wants and the uneasy restraints inseparable from a crowded population are not known, wherein we feel ourselves dependent immediately and solely on the bounty of nature, and the strength of our own arm."[28] In other words, it was the man apart from civilization's discontents who could find happiness and self-definition by virtue of his strength, cunning, and uses of nature.

In tracing the evolution of the Daniel Boone myth from John Filson's study in 1784, Slotkin turns to *Sketches of Western Adventure* by John A. McClung, published at the beginning of Jackson's second term in office in 1832. As men moved west, the Boone myth moved with them, and the result was that the famous frontiersman became more and more westernized, less of a projection of Filson's eastern aesthetic. Slotkin explains that in McClung's book the West becomes "the realm of violent adventure, in which a man's courage, prowess, and intelligence are proven in a struggle for survival against the wilderness and the savages," and Boone is "a man of action rather than thought, a man of simple rather than subtle speech, a participant in thrilling combats rather than a sensitive landscape-painter."[29] These descriptions of the West and Boone are freighted with Jacksonian overtones—the manliness ethos—and Slotkin's paraphrasing of McClung's Boone would also be an accurate rendition of the mythologized Jackson, suggesting that Boone in the 1830s became an extension of the Jacksonian mystique. Slotkin explains further that

> McClung sought to disparage Boone's pretentions to philosophic insight or literary accomplishment. Let the hunter stick to his rifle and tell only true stories of his hairbreadth escapes; leave literature to the dudes, who come to dress rough truth in the trappings of spurious poetry. McClung actually condemns Boone for falling victim to the literary blandishments of the East, and mocks his literary interest and desire for fame in the East as unworthy of his hunter's vocation. He compares Boone, the strong champion of the West, to Samson, shorn of his strength by the artful temptations of an effeminate civilization. . . . McClung's own admiration, as the rest of the text makes clear, was reserved for men who read less and took more scalps.[30]

Filson had created a Boone who spoke a lofty rhetoric; McClung wanted to de-intellectualize him, a process employed by Jacksonians in their assault on John Quincy Adams that put Andrew Jackson in the White House.

In part, Jackson's victory over Adams was a victory of action over ideas—manliness over what was accepted as its effete opposite—in a contest between "the plowman and the professor."[31] Anti-intellectualism and the anxiety it implies were a part of the egalitarian complex which not only helped install Andrew Jackson as president but took him as its symbol as well. Ward has pointed out that the material and geographic expansion of the first half of the nineteenth century "needed a philosophy less than it needed action, but Americans satisfied both needs by developing a philosophy of action. Jackson sanctified this philosophy in his own person. . . . The age of Jackson framed a philosophy that allowed it freedom of action and elected a president who provided content for the abstractions of its creed. . . . He was presented as a child of the forest and the major incidents of his career were explained in terms of this untutored genius."[32]

Like the Jacksonian version of Daniel Boone, Jackson may not have been able to articulate a fine point of logic with his social and intellectual superiors nor would he care to, but he could shoot straight, face danger and pain without flinching (e.g., his duel with Charles Dickinson), and speak from the experience of a rigorous life rather than from the innocence of a Harvard classroom. In short, Jackson brought earthy wisdom to Washington instead of esoteric knowledge and, for the first time in the history of the United States, the presidency affirmed an increasingly noticeable streak of anti-intellectualism in American life. Their independence from Europe secure, Americans turned upon themselves and found on their own eastern doorstep the cultivated, effeminate enemy of the true democrat. Thus, a vote for Jackson was not only a vote against Adams but against everything he represented in the popular mind, and their contest was described as a match between "John Quincy Adams who can write/ And Andrew Jackson who can fight."[33]

Other political and folk figures such as Davy Crockett—the Whig's rural response to the Jacksonian mystique—and, later, Abraham Lincoln, reaffirmed the belief that bookishness and refinement were poor criteria by which to judge a man's ability to meet the tough problems of a raw land. It was their coarseness, their unschooled wisdom, that were their virtues and made them mythical heroes while still alive. As a new resident on Shoal Creek in Tennessee, Crockett rose from Justice of the Peace to colonel in the militia and from there to the state legislature. In 1826 he campaigned with tall and funny tales and was elected to Congress. For Crockett and the people he represented, his abilities as a political leader were one with his abilities as a man of action, and when matters could not be settled with intimidating prowess, common sense and native wisdom would do instead:

> There were some gentlemen that invited me to go to Cambridge, where the big college or university is; where they keep ready-made titles or nicknames to give people. I would not go, for I did not know but they might stick an LL.D. on me before they let me go; and I had no idea of changing "Member of the House of Representatives of the United States," for what stands for "lazy lounging dunce," which I am sure my constituents would have translated my new title to be, knowing that I had never taken any degree, and did not own to any, except a small degree of good sense not to pass for what I was not.[34]

McClung's Boone, therefore, and other western figures like him were popular because they appealed to the westerner's Jacksonian admiration for bold, often bloodthirsty, heroes and to the easterner's appreciation for sensational narratives which reinforced the image of the westerner as a rough and violent character. And as a Jacksonian folk character, Boone held additional appeal for the times because he confirmed and justified the West as "the land of opportunity for men on the make. Boone himself had seen the West in these terms when he carved out a baronial land grant for himself and speculated unsuccessfully in land. Everything in the West was a commodity or a resource—something that could be mined, cultivated, or exploited for profit."[35] In thus assessing the western frame of mind, Slotkin also discovers conflicting psychological forces at work and the ways men attempted to resolve them:

> Behind the economic motives and aspirations of the westerners were more subtle impulses of fear and of hope....Like the Pu-

ritans, the western emigrants feared the changes that their new environment might induce and the dark impulses it might discover within them. They feared the unfamiliar surroundings; the threat of Indians; the thick, encumbering woods that isolated them from their past and their kind. However, they differed from the Puritans in some crucial respects, not the least of which was their possession of a store of historical knowledge, derived through legend and literature, of the experiences of their predecessors in the wilderness, which provided precedents for their life in the forest that their ancestors had lacked. More crucial than this was the belief of the new frontiersmen that their own individual prowess, their associated power, and the efficacy of their time-perfected technological gear (axe and rifle) made them able to contest with the forces of the natural wilderness as an equal antagonist.[36]

While the conditions of survival in the wilderness had changed little since the time of the Puritans, the motives and methods for confronting the wilderness had changed radically by the nineteenth century. The Puritans cleared the land (and the Indian from it) to build a new Eden made up of purified Christians and converted heathens, but the sons of Boone and Bumppo attacked the land to get ahead and assert their prowess, their autonomy from social and geographical restraint.

Some of the sons of America's mythical frontiersmen were the mountain men who appeared to flee civilization by crossing the Mississippi and the Great Plains to open the Rocky Mountain fur trade. They were, however, the advance guard for future capitalists who, like the mountain men themselves, would pursue their economic and social freedom with anarchic fury. As in the case of Jackson, the hero status of the mountain man was established by how the public perceived him—the apparent aptness of his response to rapid change and cultural upheaval—rather than by what he actually was. Described by Smith, the mountain man was the epitome of rugged individualism, and "his costume, his speech, his outlook on life, often enough his Indian squaw, gave him a decidedly savage aspect."[37] This "savage aspect" flaunted by the mountain man in his disdain for eastern institutions would, by the latter decades of the nineteenth century, be masked by outward gentility and the principles of social Darwinism, yet the precedent he had set would remain intact, and the urge toward primitivism as a means to an end would continue to motivate the American male long after his more colorful predecessor had been annihilated by mass migration and technology. Such primitivism was only superficial because, as Slotkin has stated, "the hunter and the western entrepreneur, the man-on-the-make, were essentially the same in their attitude toward the world and their fellows. Both relied on material success on a massive scale to prove the power of their manhood in a threatening world." And the best example of this merger between the hunter and the "speculating proto-capitalist" can be found in the legendary mountain men.[38] Thus, while they were popularly rendered either as vermin-infested white Indians or as heroic responses to the neatly ordered eastern culture, the fact of the matter was that they were not "an alternative to the money-and-status religion of Jacksonian America, but an idiosyncratic and extreme expression of its values."[39]

In his speech "To the Embodied Militia," given just before the main battle at New Orleans and at a time when geographic boundlessness tantalized the American imagination, Jackson suggested that victory relied on a particular view of nature: "Inhabitants of an opulent and commercial town, you have by a spontaneous effort shaken off the habits, which are created by wealth, and shewn that you are resolved to deserve the blessings of fortune by bravely defending them."[40] Concerning this address, Ward writes that "Jackson's thought is here stated in terms of historical primitivism. It is assumed that the advance of wealth and material well-being saps moral and physical strength. Negatively there is the implication that the condition of man in a state of nature is somehow superior. One will notice, however, that Jackson is addressing the inhabitants of an opulent and commercial town; there would be no sense in making a statement such as this to farmers from the frontier regions in Kentucky."[41] It was the popularized, mythologized Jackson and not Jackson himself who turned the Battle of New Orleans into a victory of nature over civilization, a victory suggesting that being a frontiersman, a mountain man, a westerner sprung from nature was superior to the life of civilized sluggishness led by city dwellers. And being superior, one way or another, was what men were concerned with in a new democracy they defended even as they began to fear its potential consequences. Thus, the Battle of New Orleans was not just a victory of nature over civilization, though it was certainly that, but of a certain sense of manliness over its decadent opposite.

In his *Memoirs of Andrew Jackson*, Samuel Putnam Waldo hails the War of 1812 for halting the moral and physical decay of Americans, and his meaning is clear: while Americans continued to imitate European models of class consciousness and wealth after the Revolution when the Fatherland had been officially rejected, they risked weakness and even, perhaps, a return to subjugation. But the second defeat of the British and the rise of Jacksonianism demonstrated the determination of America's sons to repulse European encroachments on their way of life once and for all.[42] For Waldo and others whose enthusiasm for Jackson led them to assess American history in European terms to justify their points of view, the War of 1812 and the exploits of the General and his army signalled the beginning of a new age because the heroes were "freeholders, or the sons of freeholders; they were not taken from the streets of dissipated and corrupt cities, or enlisted into the army to prevent their becoming victims to the shivering pangs of want."[43] The pervasiveness of this belief in the revitalized freeholder, the common man, can be seen in the fact that while there was some upward mobility, however slight, among common men in the first half of the nineteenth century compared to the more static eighteenth century, an inordinate amount of energy, activity, and movement was devoted to what they believed was possible for them as individuals. Men were thus pitted against institutions, the land, themselves, and other men in a struggle to succeed, and insofar as personal egos were involved, men on the make gave form to the masculinity cult through their actions.

The rejection of Europe and exaltation of the yeoman maintained a tradition in American thought via Crevecoeur and Jefferson and help to explain the mythical transformation of Jackson in the popular mind. In a sense, he became an updated Natty Bumppo in presidential clothing or, in the words of D. H. Lawrence describing Bumppo, "a saint with a gun."[44] This is not to say that Cooper's hero became the prototype for the American male in the nineteenth century, but only that certain qualities invested in Bumppo were held over for a new era and for new reasons, a residue of literary-historical nostalgia that, faced with a world far different from Bumppo's, caused the American male to chafe from new discomforts. In other words, democracy in the promised land held mixed blessings for the common man who felt great hope for his personal future with Old Hickory in the lead but who also sensed great danger. Jackson's "To the Embodied Militia" reveals this anxiety by indicating the morally debilitating effects of cosmopolitan wealth. To be sure, Jackson understood the Protestant work ethic as a potent force in the American consciousness, and, true to form, he expressed his belief that too much money was just as evil as too little, the ideal being a steady income somewhere in the middle.[45] This meant that those who aspired to the virtues of industry and thrift must be on the lookout for anyone or anything threatening their Yankee independence, yet without such a threat, the developing middle class would not have had an "enemy" or opposite against which they could act and thereby define themselves. They needed believable scapegoats onto which they could displace their anxiety.

Jackson and Jacksonians provided men with the adversaries they required for self-definition by campaigning against the aristocracy and the Bank and convincing the people that, in Meyers's words,

> the world of independent producers, secure in their modest competence, proud in their natural dignity, confirmed in their yeoman character, responsible masters of their fate—the order of the Old Republic—was betrayed. From the great visible centers of private wealth and power, a web of economic and political influence reached into every community, threatened every household in the land. Banks and corporations, with their paper mysteries, their secret hold on public men, their mask of anonymity, their legal untouchability, held invisible powers over the life of the community, greater even than their manifest controls.[46]

The threat was clear, and Old Hickory led the charge for all men who wished to remain powerful in their autonomy rather than become nameless victims of a small but conspiratorial crowd. Thus, a major paradox emerged in the Jacksonian mind—not articulated but revealed in attitudes and behavior—between egalitarianism on the one hand and individualism on the other, since in concept and in practice they are mutual contradictions. The Jacksonian call for a society of tough, independent citizens canceled itself out as a call for conformity, or, according to Meyers, "the ultimate sources of American character are found in that radical equality of condition which makes men masterless and separate. Everything seems possible, nothing certain, and life short."[47]

One reason, therefore, that the middle class is always rising is that those who belong to it and those who aspire to it espouse its values and virtues while they try, once the status has been secured, to escape the conformity and anonymity it enforces. Jacksonians, like men ever since, were restless to achieve something more than that which, according to the formula of hard work and moderation, they were supposed to be content with. A rich continent before them, a tradition of Yankee brashness behind them, and the threat of economic ruin within them, American males established a pattern of so-called rugged individualism, "so-called" because in fact they were, more often than not, running scared in a democracy whose great potential was also its greatest liability: all men would be free to be alike and, it followed, to be powerless. Thus, the often noted restlessness of the nineteenth-century American was more than just a simple curiosity to see what might lie beyond the next hill; it was a restlessness born of an anxiety made all the more compelling because the land and the opportunities were there to feed it. The times were filled with a frenetic activity as men threw themselves into a boundless search for wealth and self, even as they sensed the potential chaos of endless drifting from which, for all its evils, a class-ridden, status-bound society had protected them.

During his tour of the United States in 1831–1832, Alexis de Tocqueville made some telling observations in this regard:

> In the United States a man builds a house to spend his latter years in it, and he sells it before the roof is on: he plants a garden, and lets it just as the trees are coming into bearing: he brings a field into tillage, and leaves other men to gather the crops: he

embraces a profession, and gives it up: he settles in a place, which he soon afterward leaves, to carry his changeable longings else-where. If his private affairs leave him any leisure, he instantly plunges into the vortex of politics; and if at the end of a year of unremitting labor he finds he has a few days' vacation, his eager curiosity whirls him over the vast extent of the United States, and he will travel fifteen hundred miles in a few days, to shake off his happiness. Death at length overtakes him, but it is before he is weary of his bootless chase of that complete felicity which is for ever on the wing. At first sight there is something surprising in this strange unrest of so many happy men, restless in the midst of abundance. The spectacle itself is however as old as the world; the novelty is to see a whole people furnish an exemplification of it.[48]

The egalitarian myth concludes that the rise of the common man and his freedom from political and economic tyranny were the culmination of the great democratic experiment. Edward Pessen has observed that

the rise of Andrew Jackson and the other "new men" who came to the fore after the end of the Virginia Dynasty was widely regarded as the ascension of self-made men—albeit men of un-usual ability and determination—to the highest levels of govern-ment. That humble origins—actual or alleged—were all the rage in the era of "Tippecanoe and Tyler too," was a sign that the people would no longer settle for leadership by an elite. Tom, Dick, and Harry insisted on leaders in their own image. That some of these notions are sheer myth does not detract from their influence. They remain embedded in the nation's memory of its political past as a dramatic reminder of the rise of the common man.[49]

Viewed another way, egalitarianism (and thus much of pop-ularized Jacksonianism) stated that each man had the right to be like all other men, while at the same time it tormented him with the implication that to be only a part of the masses and nothing more—to be "common"—was a sure sign of weakness and complacency in a dynamic, growing republic, whose hall-mark was an unprecedented rate of change. So if men were at least free to feel equal, they were also free to despise and to fear such equality and to pursue any means of escaping it. Tocqueville observed that while the democrat may believe that he has been liberated by the attack on inherited wealth and class privilege, he has only allowed the delusion to trap him once again, since "the same quality which allows every citizen to conceive these lofty hopes, renders all the citizens less able to realize them: it circumscribes their powers on every side, while it gives freer scope to their desires." Having abolished the power of some, men face competition from everyone, and "the barrier has changed its shape rather than its position. When men are nearly alike, and all follow the same track, it is very difficult for any one individual to walk quick and cleave a way through the dense throng which surrounds and presses him."[50]

The partial comparison of Jackson and Natty Bumppo thus assumes a tension similar to the one Tocqueville discovered in American men. Bumppo was no democrat faced with the anxieties and threats of egalitarianism—indeed, he embodied Cooper's reservations about equality—but he was a simple man of nature and a deadly shot whose virtue and valor rested on these very qualities. In the early nineteenth century they are recast in the form of Andrew Jackson and his men, not to demonstrate historical fact but to make an emotional appeal to concepts long held dear by Americans. The Jacksonian male could not, however, define himself in a congenial relationship with nature no matter how hard his myth makers might try since, like it or not, he was compelled to define himself in relationship with all other men in what was threatening to become, even then, a mass society.

Men in the nineteenth century learned quickly to view and to use economic gain as a means of proving something both to themselves and to other men, namely, that money was the measure not only of the ability to endure risk and hardship but to defeat other men. In brief, the acquisition of wealth became a test among men for those who, knowing that life was short and time was money, were willing to chase the main chance with leaps and bounds, often risking all in the hope of gaining everything. Some rushed to the West for gold and furs; others challenged a different kind of economic frontier in the East, one every bit as brutal and forbidding, by gambling in industry and commerce. Keeping in mind the concept of the female super-ego in the American consciousness, what Geoffrey Gorer has noted about men and business is significant, namely, that business, along with its adjunct, politics, possesses an immunity to the constraining voice of the mother/teacher because businessmen and politicians are primarily concerned with things rather than with people, and thus their world is a peculiarly masculine one beyond the reach of feminine influence.[51] And for those who survived this world, material possessions provided the symbols of their success and prowess, a phenomenon culminating in the gaudiness of the Gilded Age among those who were the children of the Age of Jackson. The greatest of these—the Rockefellers, the Goulds, the Carnegies, et al.—would supply a male-oriented culture with heroic examples of economic dreams come true just as, some decades earlier, Andrew Jackson had supplied the popular mind with its first heroic, presidential image of the kind of man it would take to subdue and develop the new America.[52]

In this light, the essential conservatism of Jacksonianism—e.g., the sanctity of the individual and his property—cannot be ignored. Indeed, these captains of industry raised under the influence of the period would, in their own time, defend their extraordinary economic exploitation in precisely these Jacksonian, conservative terms with no thought of compromise at all. And in his own way, Andrew Jackson seemed to suit changing social and economic conditions because he possessed the particular manliness needed to meet those conditions straight on without the radical unruliness such observers as James Fenimore Cooper noted among so many common men set loose by democracy. Basically, Cooper took Jackson as the only acceptable compromise between a stifling aristocracy and a vulgar, rabid democracy and he was not being overly sensitive in this regard. Rather, he felt a key tension—identified by Erik Erikson as the "native polarity of aristocracy and mobocracy"—that helped to form the modern American identity and, along with it, the Jacksonian frame of mind.[53]

The fact that a "mobocracy" chafing against the upper class was forming with Jackson as its spokesman did not, however, mean that the Jacksonian mystique went unopposed, and by

the time of the 1828 campaign, Jackson's adversaries were denouncing both him and his popular image as a ruse, a reaction
suggesting just how threatened they were by the mystique. And
while the bitterness was not wholly unfounded, a rejection of
the mystique did not imply rejection of the assumptions behind
it, and the only real basis for complaint at all lay in the belief
that they had been improperly applied. The myth of egalitarianism was in fact so strong that in the 1840 campaign between
Harrison and Van Buren, the Whigs employed Jacksonian rhetoric to gain a decisive victory, and the *Democratic Review* lamented, "We have taught them to conquer us!" Now Harrison
was the "Cincinnatus of the West," his critics were labeled as
"Eastern officeholder pimps," and little Van was "a man who
wore corsets, put cologne on his whiskers, slept on French beds,
rode in a British coach, and ate with golden spoons from silver
plates when he sat down to dine in the White House."[54] On
both sides of the political fence, therefore, the eastern snob, the
dandy, came to be viewed as less than a man, an effeminate
weakling incapable of measuring up to the mythical manliness
of either Jackson or Harrison, as the case may be, whose toughness was ostensibly forged on the frontier.

In other instances, too, inflammatory masculine rhetoric was
employed to express social, political, and moral points of view,
and Bertram Wyatt-Brown's study of three famous men involved
in the slavery controversy indicates that the masculinity cult
cannot always be defined according to a particular philosophical
persuasion or class. Rather, it must be understood as a psychosexual, cultural phenomenon which found expression in various sectors of the society, including those at odds with each
other. Wyatt-Brown has said of his three subjects that "in their
upbringing, ideological commitments, and male identifications,
James Gordon Bennett, editor of the *New York Herald*, William
Lloyd Garrison, and John Brown exemplified different expressions of a common theme—the meaning of 19th-century American manhood."[55]

Wyatt-Brown shows that Bennett's Jacksonianism was based
on the editor's admiration for Old Hickory as "duelist, slave-
owner, Indian-fighter, horse-race gambler, enemy of effete fed-

eral bankers, foe of eastern drawing-room snobs and of abolitionist 'incendiaries.' Democrats—even Tammany Hall—often enjoyed the *Herald*'s irreverent support. So did anyone who gave expression to virile Americanism, which was Bennett's most obsessive theme."[56] From Bennett's anti-abolitionist position, various menaces could be seen such as clerical manipulation, female efforts to encroach upon male prerogatives, and threats of black restlessness in the form of sexual lust for white women and of killing white males. Bennett maintained that abolitionist, middle-class pieties would feminize the country and take away the sexual and social rights of the hard-working, Anglo-Saxon male. Women abolitionists were doubly damned as a coalition of "unsexed females," and those men, such as William Lloyd Garrison, who stood with them were accused of fighting "from behind the whalebone and cotton padding of their female allies."[57]

Concerning the slave issue, Garrison was the antithesis of Bennett, and the "muscular Christianity" he advocated was popular throughout the nineteenth century, eventually gaining one of its most famous spokesmen in Theodore Roosevelt.[58] Yet like Bennett himself, Garrison employed the sexual stereotypes of the time to push his messages: "Men of natural softness and timidity, of a sincere and effeminate virtue, will be apt to look on these bolder, hardier spirits," of the abolitionist movement "as violent, perturbed and uncharitable."[59] Unlike Bennett, however, Garrison was a traditional moralist through and through, a voice for an age that believed that masturbation would lead to insanity and that slavery was not just a political or social issue but a sexual and, therefore, a moral one as well. He thus declared that "the 16 slave states constitute one vast brothel," and that his cause was "to save a million of the gentler sex from pollution, field labor, and the lash. It is to put an end to an impure and disgraceful amalgamation."[60] It was Garrison's moral duty to oppose the evils of slavery and his manly obligation to defend the gentler sex from weak-willed, degenerate slave owners who were themselves slaves to their own desires. While his opposition to slavery is, of course, irrefutable, Garrison's choice of images is significant beyond that particular issue because they imply that one test of true manliness is the denial, or repression, of sexual urges (an aspect of nineteenth-century thought to be discussed more fully later in this study).

Unlike both Bennett and Garrison, John Brown was neither a gifted writer nor an eloquent speechmaker but a man of decisive, if crude, action who, in Kansas in the mid-1850s, discovered his life's mission—freedom for slaves. With his raid on the Harpers Ferry arsenal and his execution, Brown galvanized northern outrage, became the hero of such notable New Englanders as Theodore Parker, Thomas Wentworth Higginson, Ralph Waldo Emerson, and Henry David Thoreau, and moved the nation a crucial step away from the debating hall, closer to the battleground. Action and martyrdom, not words, made him the man of the hour: Emerson declared that those on his side were not "people of scented hair and perfumed handkerchiefs, but men of gentle blood and generosity. For what is the oath of gentle blood and knighthood? What but to protect the weak and lowly against the strong oppressor?" and Francis Lieber, a Columbia professor, scoffed that "Brown died like a man," while "Virginia fretted like a woman."[61] Wyatt-Brown concludes that while much of the American notion of manhood was only a myth, "it gave meaning to life itself and helped to mobilize armies on both sides of the Potomac. In an effort to deny cowardice, thousands went to their death. Furthermore, this cult of manliness demonstrated that events of history are sometimes determined less by actual circumstances than by the perceptions of them."[62]

Perceptions of Andrew Jackson, for instance, were often determined by his ability to maintain a delicate blend of westerner and aristocrat. This made it possible for him to inspire the popular imagination because, unlike the blue-blooded Adams who exuded eastern, highbrow refinement, Old Hickory had just enough roughness around his edges to at least appear to be what the people wanted. Thus, what has often been true in the making of cultural heroes was true in Jackson's case as well, namely, the people tended to believe what they needed to rather than what was genuinely believable so long as some evidence, however scant, corroborated their choices. Likewise, because he was far more than a country bumpkin, Jackson did not alienate all but the farmer and the frontiersman, and the fact that he was many things to many people goes some way toward explaining the massive appeal of the mystique in 1828. At various times an aristocrat and egalitarian, rich and poor, friend of the small farmer and land speculator, he could approach public concerns from several points of view and was, therefore, elected without having a recognizable platform other than militant nationalism and public access to office. Nationalism in particular was related to the manliness ethos because it was both a collective chest-thumping of the sons toward the rejected, European father-figure and an official expression of the sense of boundlessness and relentless acquisition men felt as they looked to the West.

Jackson became, in short, a cultural symbol, a mythological character embodying the manliness ethos and capturing the nation to such an extent that long after his two terms as president, the Jacksonian mystique lived on. At his death, one eulogist declared that "he wielded the axe, guided the plough, and made, with his own hands, the most of his farming utensils—as nature had made him a farmer and a mechanic, besides making him a statesman and soldier."[63] He was a man whose courage, decisiveness, and manly demeanor were attributed to his close alliance with the land, yet such tidy terms as "courage" and "decisiveness" are insufficient for a comprehension of that ethos since Andrew Jackson was not the first public figure to suggest those qualities, especially with the heroes of the Revolution still so fresh in the American memory. Instead, it was how Americans in the first half of the nineteenth century defined their terms—their cultural criteria—to fit the man to his time that promoted Jackson to the rank of cultural hero over a man such as John Quincy Adams.

Earlier it was stated that Jacksonianism sustained the Jeffersonian ideal of the self-sufficient farmer working in harmony with the landscape he inhabited and, while this is true in one sense, in another it is not the whole truth. Jefferson and Jeffersonians placed their faith in the power of the human mind— e.g., the Declaration of Independence and Jefferson's involvement in the founding of the University of Virginia—and their pursuit of the pastoral ideal was primarily an intellectual one, which even Jefferson eventually had to concede was unrealistic. To confront the realities of a dynamic, rather than a static, society, Jacksonians rejected the eighteenth-century faith in Understanding for the intuitive powers of the human heart, or Reason. These modes of perception were essentially the Transcendentalists', and the implicit acceptance of Reason over Understanding provided common men the means to support Andrew Jackson without having to examine whatever empirical evidence and neatly rhetorical objections the Whigs were able to throw against them. Also, because men's acceptance of Reason was implicit, they did not have to deal with Emerson's contention that Reason was to be equated with female, or focal, vision: the ability to see the whole instead of just the parts. This would have been untenable, and Jackson was merely assigned what were believed to be the appropriate manly attributes without any concern for what philosophers believed to be the sources of those attributes. Robust, unceremonious, and irreverent, he was simply the best man for the job, all of which indicates how, in times of cultural stress, men will often indicate their preferences according to the most elemental, emotional criteria.

The Understanding, after all, is limited to the mastery of methodical thought, of particular tasks and data, and while talent is necessary for this sort of work, it is no match for the genius of the natural man, the intuitive man, the man of Reason as many of Jackson's supporters defined it. And in 1828, the point was made for him: "He has unfortunately, perhaps for himself (but fortunately for his country), been called to act on some most trying occasions, when safety was to be found only in that bold and decided course which is ever pursued by Nature's great men, but which is far above the reach of the man of official detail," and in 1834 *The New York Times* assessed the particular quality of mind responsible for Old Hickory's success: "He arrives at conclusions with a rapidity which proves that his process is not through the tardy avenues of syllogism, nor over the beaten track of analysis, or the hackneyed walk of logical induction. For, whilst, other minds, vigorous and cultivated, are pursuing these routes, he leaves them in the distance, and reaches his object in much less time, and with not less accuracy."[64]

Regardless, therefore, of the fact that Jackson's famous victory over the British was at least part fluke, Jackson's rise to prominence was believed to be neither predestined nor accidental: it was the result of character, cast in iron and willful. Moreover, as one speechmaker said, "it is character alone, that can lift a man above accident—it is that alone which, if based upon good principles and cultivated with care, can render him triumphant over vicissitudes and prosperous even in adversity," and the proof for this lies in the truth that the Almighty "prefers, as an enticement to exertion and for the reward of prudence, to permit effects to follow their appropriate causes—to give the race to the swift and the battle to the strong."[65] By implication, then, those who could run the swiftest race to recognition, who could fight hardest the battles—literal and figurative—for survival were, by popular decree and Divine sanction, the manliest and the most virtuous of men. They had moved from the anonymity of an egalitarian mass to a higher level of recognition and power, personifying in the process the aspirations of all men who cherished equality as an ideal but feared it as a force capable of blotting them out economically and socially. Together, the cult of the self-made man and the figure of Andrew Jackson expressed the sentiment of the time by fusing a broadly based abstraction focusing on character and a living symbol of that abstraction demonstrating its efficacy. Concept and symbol flourished in a nation struggling, like its democratic citizens, to define itself amid conditions not yet clearly understood and, therefore, capable of producing anxiety:

> As a social type the man of efficient will power, the man capable of self-direction, comes to be valued when society, because of social and economic fluidity, presents its members with a variety of choices and demands a great amount of initiative. Such a social period is, of course, a period of change, a period of transition. Transition is a pallid word for what was happening to America in the period 1815 to 1845. Change was the ruling characteristic. Movement was not only westward geographically, it was upward socially. Expansion was extensive, measured by land mass, and intensive, measured by economic development.[66]

In the midst of all this flux, Jackson's call for an aggressive nationalism and public access to office underscored a major paradox faced by the Jacksonian male in his support of these issues: emotionally committed to the collective security of nationalism, he nonetheless demanded his right to rise above his fellow men on the basis of his own merits rather than privilege. One was a show of strength at the expense of the individual; the other was a test of character affirming the individual. Both were felt necessary even though they were not always compatible, and so, like Jackson himself, the Jacksonian man had to be many things, though not to as many people but to himself. The cry for equal access to offices was metaphorical rather than literal for the simple reason that even if every man had the same chance to prove himself worthy, only a few offices existed to be filled. Instead, the democrat wanted the freedom to rise economically and, as a result, socially, so that his hard-won status might distinguish him in a way that inherited status could not: worth proved via a cultural rite of passage. Thus, Jacksonian democracy did not reflect the aspirations of the working man *per se* but those of the hopeful capitalist, as the description given of American social conditions by the immigrant Francis J. Grund suggests: "Business is the very soul of an American: he pursues it, not as a means of procuring for himself and his family the necessary comforts of life, but as the fountain of all human felicity....It is as if all America were but one gigantic workshop, over the entrance of which there is the blazing inscription, 'No admission here, except on business.' "[67]

Perhaps the most significant portion of Grund's statement is his belief that the American male does not pursue profit to provide for either himself or his family but to gain happiness in the process itself, in competition that allows the best man to win and to vent his frustration over economic authority at the same time. Such was the intent of Jackson's veto message on the question of re-chartering the Bank of the United States in 1832, a message that does not show a radical urge to level society in the name of equality but to free society from authoritative, restrictive institutions:

> It is to be regretted that the rich and powerful too often bend the acts of government to their selfish purposes. Distinctions in society will always exist under every just government. Equality of talents, of education, or of wealth cannot be produced by human institutions. In the full enjoyment of the gifts of Heaven and the

> fruits of superior industry, economy, and virtue, every man is
> equally entitled to protection by law; but when the laws undertake
> to add to these natural and just advantages artificial distinctions,
> to grant titles, gratuities, and exclusive privileges, to make the
> rich richer and the potent more powerful, the humble members
> of society—the farmers, mechanics, and laborers—who have nei-
> ther the time nor the means of securing like favors to themselves,
> have a right to complain of the injustice of their government.[68]

Those who survive and prosper will do so because of "superior
industry, economy, and virtue," or, to use a popular term of
the age, character. Jackson's message is clear in its expression
of the philosophy of the rising middle class, taking as its aim
the liberation rather than the limitation of the businessman to
prosper by his own devices, to grow up, as it were, after first
being economically dependent on England, then on the dictates
of another source of power in his own land.

The war on such institutions as the Bank can, therefore, be
viewed another way, one not so much economic as psychological. Michael Paul Rogin has written that "even in good times,
large external economic institutions—bank, factory, and market
itself—gained increasing control over the conditions of existence. . . . Mobility and social dislocation fed personal anxieties
over moral worth and social place," and "market society shattered old social bonds, and made individualism, opportunity,
and self-help the cardinal values. Dissolving social boundaries
promised independence; men blamed the proliferating organi-
zations of market society for the failures of that promise."[69] A
peculiar brand of adolescent rebellion thus became a characteristic of Jacksonian economics, and Jackson saw the Bank as the
great parental enemy to be rejected, a point of view suggesting
stress displacement by which anxieties—in this case, a chafing
against the internalized female super-ego—are projected onto
other people or things to vent those anxieties. The process does
not involve direct analogies but rather indirect, or unconscious,
associations.

"The mother bank," a term used by Jackson himself,[70] was
for the WASP mind (Jackson and his closest advisors were devoted Masons) an institution trying to compromise the Protes-

tant belief in personal initiative by controlling men with a smothering maternalism, and that mind reacted against the mother-figure with much the same vehemence—short of actual war—formerly directed against the father-figure. Rogin describes a Jacksonian caricature of "the mother bank" in which she is "vomiting gold coins, holding a bottle for the pugilist Biddle (who boxes in a ring with Jackson), and sheltering hordes of little Whig and banker devils." A zealous follower of Old Hickory wrote "Kill the great monster, and the whole brood which are hatched and nourished over the land will fall an easy prey."[71] The bad children of "the mother bank" had to be destroyed so that the good children could prosper independently. Otherwise, according to Van Buren, they would conspire on behalf of the parent

> to produce throughout society a chain of dependence, to nourish in preference to the manly virtues that give dignity to human nature, a craving desire for luxurious enjoyment and sudden wealth, which renders those who seek them dependent on those who supply them; to substitute for republican simplicity and economical habits a sickly appetite for effeminate indulgence.[72]

In short, the Bank would keep men tied to institutional apron strings, unable to become economically free or, in other words, to grow up. They would be mama's boys, feminized and no more powerful than the weaker sex or the decadent sibling rivals who must be defeated because they are favored by the mother.

The battle against the Bank eventually waned, but it symbolized a popular, psychologically necessary, rejection of corporate privilege and opened the way for free enterprise, as various states permitted incorporation to all comers during the remaining decades before the Civil War. In a milieu of rapid change, the American character was developing with equal rapidity along the lines it would follow for the rest of the century. According to Hofstadter, the historical importance of the Jacksonian movement lies in the fact that "a fluid economic and social system broke the bonds of a fixed and stratified political order. . . . When Jackson left office he was the hero of the lower and middling elements of American society who believed in expanding opportunity through equal rights. . . . 'This,' exulted Calvin Colton, 'is a country of self-made men, [other] than which there can be no better in any state of society.' "[73] Men were thus coming of age by transforming external forms of power into the internalized power of self, a process supplying not only a sense of boundless freedom but certain anxieties of rootlessness as well. Furthermore, the child who had to break free of the parent would, in time, become that parent himself, and after the Civil War when massive industrialism and the final assault on the West were initiated, the Jacksonian principle of free enterprise and its corollary, aggressive acquisition, would be taken up by the children of the Age of Jackson and applied with a vengeance. This time, however, they would act not to bring down the barriers of restraint but to contain the fluid chaos they had lived through and the free-floating anxieties they felt.

In ante-bellum America as the culture became more complex and males moved beyond the home to make a living, a marked ambivalence developed in young men toward the mother-figure. As a necessary part of their parental duty, mothers functioned as the super-ego for their sons, inculcating in them the discipline, training, and values needed to survive in the world at large. Yet that world also rewarded the assertion of the ego, and the male, therefore, at some point felt compelled to reject maternal influence, whether it be the symbolically maternal Bank or the actual mother, the cultural repository of Christian piety and restraint. And having been taught the value of machine-like efficiency and faced with a land only technology could truly tame, the self-made man developed his sense of self, his masculine ego, based in part on his response to and uses of nature and the machine. His ancestors had escaped the religious and legal tyrannies of Europe to establish on this continent another England, a New England in which they could do as they wished. What they could not envision at the time was a massive continent with no past to define it and a wilderness capable of crushing any efforts to control it.

The first Americans had, in effect, fled the institutional oppression of the old country only to face what must have seemed the limitless power of nature in the new land, and it was not until the nineteenth century that the descendants of those Americans were able to comprehend the potential future nature offered as well as the ways to pursue it without surrender. This meant the use of machines, which, like the nature they were turned against, possessed the capacity for tyranny. Erikson explains nature and the machine as the two autocratic forces challenging the American in the last century and in mastering them both, he became the self-made man and ego:

> In America nature is autocratic, saying, "I am not arguing, I am telling you." The size and rigor of the country and the importance of the means of migration and transportation helped to create and to develop the identity of autonomy and initiative, the identity of him who is "going places and doing things."...It is no coincidence, then, that psychological analyses should find at the bottom of much specific mental discomfort the complex of having abandoned the mother and of having been abandoned by her. In general, Americans do not experience "this country" as a "motherland" in the soft, nostalgic sense of "the old country." "This country" is loved almost bitterly and in a remarkably unromantic and realistic way....In thus mastering with a vengeance the expanses of a vast continent, Americans also learned to control the second autocrat, which was unexpectedly met with by the free sons: the machine.[74]

THE MASCULINE MACHINE

The union of men and machines against nature first occurred before the Gilded Age because America had reached a crucial period in its economic development during the years 1840–1860, a time W. W. Rostow describes as the "take-off" when the forces of economic progress "expand and come to dominate the society."[75] The primary symbol for this domination was the locomotive, a machine "associated with fire, smoke, speed, iron, and noise....It appears in the woods, suddenly shattering the harmony of the green hollow, like a presentiment of history bearing down on the American asylum."[76] Leo Marx is concerned here with an incident in Nathaniel Hawthorne's life in 1844, but his image of the locomotive has cultural significance, too, and Marx explains that Hawthorne's "The Celestial Railroad" is a "wonderfully compact satire on the prevailing faith in progress" because "in the popular culture of the period the railroad was a favorite emblem of progress—not merely technological progress, but the overall progress of the race."[77]

In retrospect, the violation of nature with machinery in nineteenth-century America appears as an inevitable phenomenon, a predictable result of the processs of civilization, predictable because men, historically tied to civilization—its systems and constraints—have periodically fled to nature to indulge in a self-saving primitivism. In literature, this impulse sends Rip Van Winkle to the mountains, Thoreau to Walden Pond, Ishmael to sea, and Huckleberry Finn over the back fence, yet in the end each returns to the town or to the shore because, among other things, they have discovered that nature is, at best, a temporary stay against civilization and, at worst, a world filled with terrors all its own. In nature, as Marx has suggested, "the superfluities and defense of everyday life are stripped away, and men regain contact with essentials. . . . What finally enables us to take the idea of a successful 'return to nature' seriously is its temporariness. It is a journey into the desert and back again."[78] The "essentials" our literary heroes often discover "out there" are not just those of unrestrained nature but of unrestrained machines and other men in nature, a "sense of the machine as a sudden, shocking intruder upon a fantasy of idyllic satisfaction. It invariably is associated with crude, masculine aggressiveness in contrast with tender, feminine, and submissive attitudes traditionally attached to the landscape."[79] Our literary heroes have heard the train's whistle across the pond, seen the try-works on the whaling ship, and witnessed the steamboat churning out of the night to swamp a fragile raft.

The men who wielded the machines were seeking a sublimated, secular salvation—primarily psychosexual—by invading and plundering nature, thereby asserting masculine dominance over her as well as the weaker, feminine portions of civilization itself. In Gorer's words, "America in its benevolent, rich, idealistic aspects is envisaged (by Americans) as feminine; it is masculine only in its grasping and demanding aspects. The American land itself—Columbia in an older iconography—is feminine; its possession has been on occasion wooing, on occasion seduction,

and on occasion rape."[80] And while these were men who utilized
the practical applications of science and who, after the Civil War,
would espouse the latest theories of Darwin and Spencer, they
were religious men, too, and they carried on, however unconsciously, ample Protestant precedent. The Puritans fled from the
decadent institutions of civilized Europe to gain their salvation
in the New Eden, yet once in the garden of the New World,
they civilized it by driving out the Indian, establishing their own
institutions, and regulating society with rigid, theocratic laws
enforced by those men most spiritually fit to govern. Another
Pilgrim, Bunyan's Christian in *Pilgrim's Progress*, flees the city
of Destruction to find salvation: "...the man began to run: now
he had not run far from his own door, when his wife and children, perceiving it, began to cry after him to return; but the man
put his fingers in his ears, and ran on, crying, Life, life eternal
life! So he looked not behind him, but fled towards the middle
of the plain."[81]

Neither civilization nor women could restrain these men from
their search for salvation, and nineteenth-century American
Protestants were no different. Filled with the expansive energy
of the age, encouraged by laissez-faire economics, and armed
with great machines as masculine extensions of themselves, they
overwhelmed nature—especially the West—with the blessings
of both God and government. This lunge into the primitive land
was a rite of passage for the masculinity cult, one in which men
attempted to prove themselves worthy of society's rewards and
superior to the effeminate gentility and high culture they despised. Thus, nature was both a refuge for wildlife and a victim
of it in what amounted to technological warfare to secure what
she offered and to defeat what she represented: wealth in the
first instance, anti-masculine qualities in the second. Such applications of technology meant progress, and Marx takes as com-
monplace that

> everyone knows that the great majority of Americans welcomed
> the new technology. As Perry Miller said, welcomed is too weak
> a verb: they grasped and panted and cried for it. Again and again,
> foreign travelers in this period testify to the nation's obsessive
> interest in power machinery. The typical American, says Michael

Chevalier, "has a perfect passion for railroads; he loves them . . . as a lover loves his mistress." In the words of another Frenchman, Guillaume Poussin, "the railroad, animated by its powerful locomotive, appears to be the personification of the American. The one seems to hear and understand the other—to have been made for the other—to be indispensable to the other."[82]

Both foreigners' observations are significant for what they imply about men and machines: in Chevalier's case, their relationship reveals the sublimation of male sexual energy; in Poussin's, they are the combined halves of a single being, each responding to the other and sharing a common purpose.

In literature, *Moby-Dick* provides one of the best analogies of the merger of man and machine. The mission of the *Pequod* was profit, the try-works its soul, and Ahab—willful, ruthless, self-possessed—turned the ship to his own design and seized the imaginations of his men with his power and his gold. They were men united against nature, and their leader, who compares himself to the precision and power of machinery ("my one cogged circle fits into all their various wheels, and they revolve"), looks astern at the ship's wake:

The path to my fixed purpose is laid with iron rails, whereon my soul is grooved to run. Over unsounded gorges, through the rifled hearts of mountains, under torrents' beds, unerringly I rush! Naught's an obstacle, naught's an angle to the iron way![83]

The nineteenth-century emphasis on character of a particular kind—expansive, self-reliant, aggressive—meant, of course, that whatever qualities constituted its opposite were at best unworthy, at worst unmasculine. Ironically, as Erikson points out, mothers developed in their sons the character traits necessary for the age, but they also were unavoidably preparing those sons to reject the maternal figure and the qualities women represented in their cultural roles. Thus, dependency, timidity, not to mention an aesthetic sensibility suggesting idleness, were considered by many men to be female attributes, and once men began either uprooting the family to challenge the actual, geographical frontier or leaving the home to struggle in the other, economic frontier, the division of roles and character traits solidified for the century. Anti-intellectual and pragmatic, this willed bifurcation to meet cultural imperatives is placed by Ward in the mainstream of Jacksonian America:

> Perhaps the most severe condemnation that can be made of nine-teenth-century America is that it equated charity and love with a lack of manhood. With the symbol of Jackson we are in the midst of the tradition which would divide life into two parts, one the province of the home, the other that of the practical world. By making the women and children of the society the guardians of virtue, the male was released to act amorally in the world outside the home, but at a large price. The male became simply an adjunct to the home. He was relegated to a function in which virtue, appreciation of the arts, or leisure time had no organic part. The woman also paid a price although at first, being en-throned, she seemed to be favored.[84]

Men thus threw themselves together in a paradoxical struggle to distinguish themselves from each other by whatever means possible, a doctrine of equal but separate by which they praised their freedom to do so even as they feared their freedom to fail: a mass of isolated men leading what Thoreau called in *Walden* "lives of quiet desperation."[85] For them, Jackson symbolized strength and determination, but his example placed a heavy burden on the individual because whichever frontier he chose, nature or business, would demand of him tremendous effort made all the more difficult by his isolation. His hope, therefore, and the hope of ante-bellum America, lay in an energy as psychic as it was physical, as spiritual as it was emotional. For God had blessed Andrew Jackson, and He would bless those who followed Jackson's example with prosperity through expansion and conquest. As Ward states, "Jackson as symbol was not the creation of Andrew Jackson from Tennessee, or of the Democratic party. The symbol was the creation of the times. To describe the early nineteenth century as the age of Jackson misstates the matter. The age was not his. He was the age's."[86] That is, if Jackson and his immediate followers were obsessed, anxiety ridden, over such issues as class privilege and the Bank, then so were many of their fellow white Protestants, the economic and political conservatives of the age. Or as Elizabeth Fox-Genovese has written, "If intrapsychic conflict should be accepted as an important feature of historical process—and I believe that it should—then, surely, it must rest its claim upon universality. The psychological mainsprings of Jackson's remarkable achievement must be what he holds in common with other men, not what differentiates him from them."[87] And if the Age of Jackson was indeed an age of anxiety, then that anxiety was universally felt—i.e., by women as well as men—and thus the relationship between the sexes was not just a battle but in various ways also a compact struck for mutual relief and security.

2

THE FEMALE FOIL

From the Age of Jackson on, the American male has attempted to define himself in an adversary relationship with other men, the culture at large, and nature, all overlapping in an anxiety-ridden snarl, which, by the end of the century, manifested itself in the compulsive and self-serving behavior of the Gilded Age. Sanctioned by Jacksonian notions of equality and laissez-faire economics, he competed with other men to rise above them, while his ruthless assault on nature was made possible in part by technology and licensed by the doctrine of manifest destiny and, somewhat later, by the more sophisticated rationalizations of social Darwinism. As suggested earlier, the treatment of the Indian and the black were symptomatic of the white male's distrust or, more accurately, his fear of primitive, unrestrained nature even though he needed these "enemies" and nature herself to define his own role against them. But the American male, like males everywhere, did not live in a social and sexual vacuum—a world without women—and the treatment of and attitudes toward the opposite sex in the nineteenth century indicate the pervasive influence of the masculinity cult in American culture.

Alexis de Tocqueville observed of American males that "in the heart of this society, so policed, so prudish, so sententiously unreal and virtuous, one encounters a complete insensibility, a sort of cold and implacable egoism when it's a question of the American indigenies.... This world belongs to us, add they.... The true proprietors of this continent are those who know how to take advantage of its riches," and while a man might suffer extreme hardships to make a dollar, "that one should do such things through curiosity, that's something that doesn't reach his intelligence... that one has a high regard for great trees and a beautiful solitude, that's entirely incomprehensible to him."[1] According to Tocqueville, this immunity to aesthetics and the concurrent desire to exploit the land helped to mold the male's attitude toward his wife and family and, obsessed with making his way in a country that freed him to do so, "the emigrant has finally created for himself an altogether individual existence. Family sentiments have come to fuse themselves in a vast egoism, and it is doubtful if in his wife and children he sees anything else than a detached portion of himself."[2] She must give so that he might receive, and Tocqueville supplies this image of the frontier wife:

> In her prematurely pale face and shrunken limbs, it is easy to see that existence has been a heavy burden for her. It is in fact, this frail creature who has already found herself exposed to unbelievable miseries. To devote herself to austere duties, submit herself to privations which were unknown to her, embrace an existence for which she was not made, such was the occupation of the finest years of her life, such have been for her the delights of marriage.... Around this woman crowd half naked children... veritable sons of the wilderness. From time to time their mother throws on them a look of melancholy and joy. To see their strength and her weakness one would say that she had exhausted herself, giving them life, and that she does not regret what they have cost her.[3]

Given the Frenchman's sense of gallantry and pity (e.g., "this frail creature") which in itself could be taken as a form of male condescension, Tocqueville's portrait of the western wife suggests as much about the husband as it describes about her, and the connections are not limited to those who left the East. Rather, Tocqueville maintained that the psychology of the pioneer male could be traced to those who remained in the East or, conversely, "the man you left in New York you find again in almost impenetrable solitudes...same clothes, same attitude, same language, same habits, same pleasures...the spirit of equality has spread a singularly even coloring over the inner habits of life. Now, note this well, it is precisely these same men who each year go to people the wilderness."[4] It would seem that democracy, with its implied threat of leveling all men to a monolithic society of shared equality, drove men to excel no matter what the cost to themselves and to their families. Yet, ironically, they shared as a means to this end a common opinion of women that enabled them to pursue individuality from a collective point of view and to believe in democracy as the surest method for determining who held sway over whom. The fittest would survive at the expense of all others and thus, as G. J. Barker-Benfield has written, "democracy marched inexorably into the forest. The representative American...compelled himself pitilessly to the destruction of the Indian and the exploitation of nature, his wife, and perhaps himself."[5] But democracy, whatever it may have meant to the individual of the time, cannot fully account for the separation of the sexes and the resultant domination of one over the other. The root cause was psychosexual, but other factors—cultural and often economic—heightened what was to become not only the separation but the battle of the sexes.

America in the first half of the nineteenth century underwent radical changes. Beginning with the Louisiana Purchase in 1803 and the Lewis-Clark expedition shortly thereafter, the nation's boundaries (and thus its collective imagination) moved far beyond the horizon, and within a couple of decades the belief in limitless space and wealth had stirred the restless spirit of a country still in its youth and brimming with energy. Americans had passed several tests of their ability to endure as a nation, and the rewards of their newly found freedom—enhanced as they were by the spirit of Jacksonianism—turned American males into a collective adolescent who, set loose at last from parental domination, proceeds to fragment himself in every possible direction in a frenzied, often destructive, binge toward self-ful-

fillment. In assessing American culture through literature, Leslie
Fiedler states in *Love and Death in the American Novel* that

> for better or worse and for whatever reasons, the American novel
> is different from its European prototypes, and one of its essential
> differences arises from its chary treatment of women and of sex.
> To write, then, about the American novel is to write about the
> fate of certain European genres in a world of alien experience. It
> is not only a world where courtship and marriage have suffered
> a profound change, but also one in the process of losing the
> traditonal distinctions of class; a world without a significant his-
> tory or a substantial past; a world which had left behind the terror
> of Europe not for the innocence it dreamed of, but for new and
> special guilts associated with the rape of nature and the exploi-
> tation of dark-skinned people; a world doomed to play out the
> imaginary childhood of Europe.[6]

The significance of this phenomenon was as great as the conditions that caused it, conditions allowing the nation to indulge
itself economically and geographically. In this regard, the transportation revolution between 1815 and 1860 did more than anything else to alter the economics and lifestyles of the American
people as steamboats, canals, and the railroad provided men
the means to move far and quickly while encouraging a psychology of aggressive adventure in search of the main chance,
wherever it might be.[7]

Divorced from Europe and without a past, institutions, or
traditions to guide them, Americans stood with their backs to
the East, their eyes to the West and the future, and those who
could move quickest, either literally or with investments or both,
would have the advantage. This much economic and geographic
mobility, occurring as it did with the rising industrialism, irrev-
ocably altered the social and family structures of American life
by sending the male outside the home and, in the process, rendering it something other than the self-sustaining economic unit
it had once been. The duties of making a living and rearing
children, formerly shared by man and woman with the patriarchal male as the final authority in matters economic and moral,
were divided, and the male—biologically, legally, and economically superior—moved away from the home, leaving behind the

female whose matriarchal power was necessarily limited to household morality. By 1870 when working women and girls were first included in the federal census, four-fifths of them were employed in traditional jobs on the farm or in domestic service, and those who did enter industry remained in unskilled positions for low wages. And while the number of women in industry increased between 1850 and the end of the century, the proportion of females to males declined during that period, a trend attributable to the fact that not only did men want to keep women out of the marketplace but that women acquiesced.[8] And they acquiesced for one of two reasons: either they never seriously questioned their status given the cultural conditioning they had experienced from girlhood on, or if they did question that status, they had limited opportunities to do much else but acquiesce in a male-oriented society.

It must be remembered that what guidelines the nineteenth century obeyed were for the most part Christian and Protestant, and they achieved mythical proportions not just during the relatively brief history of America but over centuries of cultural reinforcement and reflection. Indeed, the nineteenth-century male-female dichotomy in America can be traced to the Garden of Eden itself where, in a secular and psychological sense, the separation first occurred. Even then, Eve was an extension of Adam placed on earth for his benefit, not hers, and in her unfortunate effort to gain more than she should, she doomed all of Christendom to a life of anxiety and the struggle to survive outside the sensual and abundant Garden where she and Adam had lived naked and unashamed. For Eve had betrayed not only God and herself but Adam as well, her foolishness condemning them both to clothing, repressed sexuality, and the necessity of hard work to support themselves and their children. Thus, domesticity and sexuality based on fear and guilt were their punishment as well as their legacy to all who followed until, by the nineteenth century, those judgments handed down by God to the first couple had become the most commonly cited characteristics of the Victorian Age.

In a word, Adam and Eve had been civilized. Or at least in their forced journey from the Garden they took mankind's first reluctant steps toward civilization, its basic institution—the family—and its discontents. The initial mistake was Eve's, and only after she had eaten of the forbidden fruit did she invite Adam to join her, establishing in this event the classical encounter between a woman allied with hostile nature (the snake and the tree) and a man who must choose either to succumb and through his weakness fall or to resist and thereby establish his superiority over her as well as his right to partake further of the wealth and pleasures of the Garden: a confrontation repeated countless times in the literature, lore, and mythologies of the western world until it had become an unconscious, archetypal situation reenacted with a peculiarly American variation on the theme.

Eve, laden with guilt for her act and made aware of her own gullibility in not recognizing evil for what it was, gave herself over to Adam, bore his children, and tended his home. Adam, questioned by God and held responsible for both their sins, accepted his punishment and became an Old Testament patriarch who lived by the sweat of his brow and fathered sons to follow him. Psychologically, these prototypes—submissive and dominant, reliant and paternal, self-effacing and aggressive—were brought to the New World intact by strict Protestants whose lives were ruled by the awareness of sin and guilt on the one hand, the necessity of hard work on the other. The first American society was controlled by a male hierarchy, and that, remaining constant until well into the twentieth century, has provided men with their visible proof of power in politics, economics, social institutions, the church, and the culture at large, but it is the nature of that power and not the forms it took that might be understood here, and during the nineteenth century male resentment toward women—at the core a sexual fear and loathing since men and women are, in the most elemental sense, distinctive sexual beings—gained its fullest and most overt expression. Adam had been given Eve for companionship, and American males revealed in their attitudes and actions an unconscious belief that he would have been better off alone.

Democratic individualism, for all it offered men in terms of vertical and horizontal mobility, posed an unprecedented threat to male superiority, which, if that freedom was to be realized, had to be answered. It was an implied threat rather than an actual one since the concepts of democracy and equality were in no way intended literally to include women. Yet the implication was clear enough because democracy, at least in theory, created an atmosphere or spirit of equality capable of undermining men's efforts to rise among men without hinderance or competition from women. Regarding this egalitarian phenomenon, Tocqueville overstated the case when he claimed that it brought men and women into contact on the same level and that "equality of conditions has swept away all the imaginary, or the real, barriers which separated man from woman."[9] He makes clear, however, that equality and the institutions it fosters—e.g., marriage freely entered into by both partners—creates stricter mores rather than more lenient ones, and "the rigour of the Americans arises in part from this cause. They consider marriage as a covenant which is often onerous, but every condition of which the parties are strictly bound to fulfill, because they knew all those conditions beforehand, and were perfectly free not to have contracted them."[10] With the class barriers down (but not the legal ones since men made laws to protect themselves in the world outside the home), the sexual distinction was the only one left to the male, and he used it to erect barriers out of an age-old resentment of what women could do if, once again, male and female were to stand together naked and unashamed. Women had to be disarmed and devalued so that once they freely joined themselves to men, as Tocqueville explains,

> the independence of women is irrecoverably lost in the bonds of matrimony: if an unmarried woman is less constrained there than elsewhere, a wife is subjected to stricter obligations. The former makes her father's house an abode of freedom and of pleasure; the latter lives in the home of her husband as if it were a cloister.... Religious peoples and trading nations entertain peculiarly serious notions of marriage: the former consider the regularity of woman's life as the best pledge and most certain sign of the purity of her morals; the latter regard it as the highest security for the order and prosperity of the household. The Americans are at the same time a puritanical people and a commercial nation: their religious opinions, as well as their trading habits, consequently lead them to require much abnegation on the part of women, and a constant sacrifice of her pleasures to her duties which is seldom demanded of her in Europe. Thus in the United States the inex-

orable opinion of the public carefully circumscribes women within the narrow circle of domestic interests and duties, and forbids her to step beyond it.... It may be said that she has learned by the use of her independence, to surrender it without a struggle and without a murmur when the time comes for making the sacrifice.... Voluntarily and freely does she enter upon this engagement. She supports her new condition with courage, because she chose it.[11]

Given Tocqueville's observations, it might be said that the restrictions placed on women were not devised by men at all, but this was not the case. Women chose to accept them; they did not create them. Democracy in America was defined by white, Protestant men, and roles, rights, and privileges were assigned accordingly: blacks, Indians, and women all lacked the vote, property, and for the most part, access to higher education and training that would enable them to compete with men for jobs and money. In her study of science as masculine knowledge and of the threat to males posed by women who might want to share that knowledge, Janice Law Trecker concludes that higher learning was reserved for the masculine alliance:

However expressed, the underlying aim of the scientific conservatives was to suppress and to direct female individuality and talent into the socially acceptable channels of domestic, idealized womanhood and away from the disciplines which might increase her dangerous individuality and her knowledge of the crucial studies—i.e., the sciences. Having so recently secured the individuality of their own sex through such novelties as male suffrage, the 19th century rise in affluence, mass education and the escape from subsistence farming, conservative men were uncertain and frightened of the next step. In the new Faustian bargain, the masculine half of humanity would be given individuality and power through science, technology and abstract thought, while the feminine half of humanity would, in exchange, remain tied to nature, the race and reproduction. No longer was his pattern the farmer, tied to home and soil, but the industrialist, the worker, the craftsman, the scientist, dependent not on nature but on the new mysteries of trade, capital and technology. This new masculine freedom would have to be purchased, and the price was the sacrifice of woman's individuality. Her willingness to be submerged in duties for the sake of the family, the state and the species was the condition of his emergence as the new man of the 19th century.[12]

Outside the home, the WASP male held dominion over other males because they were not white, and in the home he claimed his traditional Christian authority over women because they were not male: an irrefutable, sexual distinction.

This distinction in turn created new and necessary barriers separating the sexes into their respective roles and playing out the Edenic legacy of sexual repression and, as a result, sublimation. Tocqueville explains that almost all men in America either entered business, politics, or some other calling outside the home while their wives, limited economically, stayed back to attend to domestic details, and this division of duties, keeping men and women apart, made "the solicitations of the one less frequent and less ardent—the resistance of the other more easy."[13] Certainly, unrestrained sex—again, naked and unashamed—was no longer possible after the Fall, and in a cultural sense, too, it was freighted with guilt of another kind because it would impede what, in the nineteenth century, had become the passwords for an age: progress, order, success. This "state of things causes lamentable cases of individual hardship, but it does not prevent the body of society from being strong and alert; it does not destroy family ties, or enervate the morals of the nation. Society is endangered not by the great profligacy of a few, but by laxity of morals among all."[14] Thus, the neurotic or, in Tocqueville's words, "tumultuous and constantly harassed life which equality makes men lead" became a pathological necessity because it "distracts them from the passion of love, by denying them time to indulge in it, but it diverts them from it by another more secret but more certain road":

> All men who live in democratic ages more or less contract the ways of thinking of the manufacturing and trading classes; their minds take a serious, deliberate, and positive turn; they are apt to relinquish the ideal, in order to pursue some visible and proximate object, which appears to be the natural and necessary aim of their desires. Thus the principle of equality does not destroy the imagination, but lowers its flight to the level of the earth. No

men are less addicted to reverie than the citizens of a democracy; and few of them are ever known to give way to those idle and solitary mediations which commonly precede and produce the great emotions of the heart. It is true they attach great importance to procuring for themselves that sort of deep, regular, and quiet affection which constitutes the charm and safeguard of life, but they are not apt to run after those violent and capricious sources of excitement which disturb and abridge it. I am aware that all this is only applicable in its full extent to America....[15]

Sex, a violent disruption of and a chaotic distraction from the affairs of men, was neutralized and so, therefore, was woman's role in the lives of men. In place of mature, passionate heterosexual love, men sought that "deep, regular, and quiet affection" described by Tocqueville above and suggestive of those things provided by a mother rather than a wife, namely, consolation and correction. Her sexuality nonexistent in the eyes of the boy, taboo in the man's, she was abstracted into a symbol of virtue, an asexual guardian of morality to whom the man could turn after dealing with the immoral world beyond the home. Barbara Welter says as much in her discussion of the cult of True Womanhood as it emerged in the 1820s:

> Woman, in the cult of True Womanhood presented by the women's magazines, gift annuals and religious literature of the nineteenth century, was the hostage in the home. In a society where values changed frequently, where fortunes rose and fell with frightening rapidity, where social and economic mobility provided instability as well as hope, one thing at least remained the same—a true woman was a true woman, wherever she was found. If anyone, male or female, dared to tamper with the complex of virtues which made up True Womanhood, he was damned immediately as an enemy of God, of civilization and of the Republic. It was a fearful obligation, a solemn responsibility, which the nineteenth-century American woman had—to uphold the pillars of the temple with her frail white hand.[16]

She was thus contained and the male, with a heightened sense of masculinity, subjected himself to the torments and temptations of the working world to illuminate her purity by contrast and to shield her from the inevitable corruption of the marketplace.

In a culture based on work and religion, men could indulge freely in both by restricting their women from one while holding them responsible for the other, and women were further circumscribed by the fact that men paid tribute to woman's power even as they limited it. Tocqueville wrote that "in the United States men seldom compliment women, but they daily show how much they esteem them," a trait he felt was opposite to the European male's excessive use of flattery as a means of expressing his contempt for women.[17] A compliment is, more often than not, a mild expression of sexual attraction and if, in withholding it, the male offers esteem in its place, he has in effect declared the woman's role in his world sexually nonfunctional and honorific. And this, too, is a disguised form of contempt in much the same way that an honorary degree for public service is conferred on someone by professionals who would never consider that person a true colleague: everyone feels good but no one is threatened or hurt in the process.

The problem, therefore, confronting women in the nineteenth century was one of self-identification, of retaining a sense of femaleness apart from assigned roles. Yet it would be inaccurate to generalize that women were totally helpless creatures, subsumed by the culture and without recourse or feeling the need for it. Catharine Beecher, for example—woman's advocate and member of a family whose influence spanned the century—was an important representative of countless, dynamic women, and she never forgot her female identity if for no other reason than the fact that men constantly reminded her of it by relegating her to a secondary social status when she desired a primary one. According to Kathryn Kish Sklar, during the course of Beecher's lifetime "she accumulated a tremendous amount of animus against male cultural dominance, but she usually expressed this anger indirectly. Her political assumptions led her to oppose the women's rights movement. Nevertheless her efforts to overcome the marginal status allotted to women constituted a central theme in her career. It caused her to innovate, to seek new channels of cultural influence, and to design an ideology that gave women a central place in national life."[18] Beecher believed that the home

and the family were the key to harmonizing such national interests as stability and order while at the same time satisfying
people's, especially women's, individual needs. Her career is
thus marked by her effort to achieve both cultural cohesiveness
and female hegemony. This was, of course, no mean task because "as American culture developed new forms of self-reali-
zation in the nineteenth century...it attached a male label to
these experiences and called women selfish and unnatural if they
wanted the same set of personal goals. For them another set
applied: devotion and service to others, selflessness, sacrifice."[19]

Beecher and women like her took these cultural prerequisites
for true womanhood and turned them into human assets, rather
than just female qualities, so that self-sacrifice might be seen as
a high calling and a benefit to society as a whole. Because people
in a democracy were free to exercise their own wills and to
pursue their own ends, often at the expense of others, moral
leadership and democratic morality required exceptional people
who were willing to set aside personal enjoyment for the sake
of others. This was Beecher's definition of benevolence and while
it expressed a negative concept of personal fulfillment—i.e., self-
denial—it was nonetheless the opposite of selfishness and provided satisfaction via voluntary restraint.[20] Regarding this concept of self-sacrifice, Sklar has noted that "as a conservative
social theory it was unparalleled, and as a means of establishing
the moral leadership of women it was ingenious, for it rewarded
most those whose restraint was greatest. Self-sacrifice became a
kind of grand achievement, and a goal worthy in its own right
as well as a means of promoting the greatest social happiness.
In the 1850s Catharine concluded that no act was moral if it was
not an act of self-sacrifice and that moral rectitude consisted
wholly in self-sacrifice."[21]

In an attempt to counter male cultural autonomy, Beecher did
not attack male power directly but subverted it by claiming that
men without women and the homes they tended were morally
bankrupt no matter how much worldly wealth they may accu-
mulate. She thus made the domestic sphere essential to the
health of the culture in her recognition of what many men were
about in the nineteenth century: they "labour diligently," she
wrote, "for the general interests of men, and forget their own

vineyard, in the heart and in the family circle, where rank weeds are speedily discovered," and any man such as this "awakens the suspicion that all his efforts for the public good are the offspring of a desire for notoriety and the praise of men."[22] The home was the moral center of the culture, and men who recognized this would turn to their women for the particular power they lacked in themselves and could not find in the world at large. Beecher's domestic ideology was a workable method for raising the value of women in and to the culture while simultaneously questioning masculine ideology. By offering an alternative to a society run by and for men, she was in effect recognizing that such a world existed but that it could also be changed to the betterment of all.

By and large, male reaction to Beecher's philosophy was favorable, unlike the denunciations aimed at the militant feminists who worked for equal rights, the vote, and direct involvement in social and political affairs. Nathaniel Hawthorne's *The Blithedale Romance*—published in 1852 when the feminist movement had just begun to stir—includes an exchange between Hollingsworth and Zenobia concerning the inequality of the sexes, and it suggests Hawthorne's own interest in reform even as it reveals a deep ambivalence over the "woman question." In fact, it is difficult to tell what unnerves Hawthorne more, Zenobia's zealous declaration of independence or Hollingsworth's brute response. She swears that "If I live another year, I will lift up my own voice in behalf of woman's wider liberty" because, she continues, "The mistrust and disapproval of the vast bulk of society throttles us, as with two gigantic hands at our throats!"[23] And Hollingsworth's response to her question "Do you despise woman?" captures the masculine ideology of the age:

> "Despise her? No!" cried Hollingsworth, lifting his great shaggy head and shaking it at us, while his eyes glowed almost fiercely. "She is the most admirable handiwork of God, in her true place and character. Her place is at man's side. Her office, that of the sympathizer; the unreserved, unquestioning believer; the recognition, withheld in every other manner, but given, in pity, through woman's heart, lest man should utterly lose faith in himself; the echo of God's own voice, pronouncing, 'It is well done!' All the separate action of woman is, and ever has been,

and always shall be, false, foolish, vain, destructive of her own best and holiest qualities, void of every good effect, and productive of intolerable mischiefs!...As true as I had once a mother whom I loved, were there any possible prospect of woman's taking the social stand which some of them—poor, miserable, abortive creatures, who only dream of such things because they have missed woman's peculiar happiness, or because nature made them really neither man nor woman!—if there were a chance of their attaining the end which these petticoated monstrosities have in view, I would call upon my own sex to use its physical force, that unmistakable evidence of sovereignty, to scourge them back within their proper bounds! But it will not be needful. The heart of true womanhood knows where its own sphere is, and never seeks to stray beyond it!" (pp. 139–40)

Certainly Hollingsworth's polemic against female equality is seen as excessive by Hawthorne and all but the most hardened readers, arising as it does out of that character's monomaniacal belief in brotherhood, which, ironically, has rendered him insensitive to the needs and beliefs of others. Yet it is Zenobia— the dark, sensual, headstrong woman—who must die, not Hollingsworth, and so she, like another of Hawthorne's women before her, has paid for her recklessness. In *The Scarlet Letter*, Hester Prynne, not Dimmesdale, must suffer the community's scorn and punishment for her sensual sin, and only by repressing her sexuality and submitting herself to public judgment can she hope to save herself from herself. Hester, unlike Zenobia, does not choose to declare herself a free woman and comes to believe that if a female prophet is to "establish the whole relation between man and woman on a surer ground of mutual happiness," that woman will have to be "lofty, pure, and beautiful," her wisdom gained through "the ethereal medium of joy."[24] In a word, she must be asexual.

Some two hundred years later, Zenobia would attempt to deliver her sex but, failing to accept the criteria set forth by Hawthorne through Hester, the feminist of *The Blithedale Romance* meets with a grisly end at the bottom of a river, and Coverdale, seeing that the recovered corpse has stiffened in the kneeling position, hopes in vain that she might have repented her sensual and free-thinking ways. Hester was the seductress in the woods who caused Dimmesdale to fall and to lose his effectiveness as a leader in society; Zenobia in her first meeting with Coverdale causes him to imagine her as a "fine, perfectly developed figure, in Eve's earliest garment" and to feel "an influence breathing out of her such as we might suppose to come from Eve" (pp. 44–45). For their Edenic sensuality, both women must suffer, one through repression and repentence, the other through despair and death.

For men, therefore, Catharine Beecher's home-as-moral-sanctuary corroborated their belief that women were best suited for domestic and moral housekeeping and so far as their understanding of her went, they were quite right. "It may not have been deliberate," Sklar writes, "but it was surely significant that all Catharine Beecher's examples of failed domestic virtue were men. Women, she assumed, were perforce versed in the arts of domestic virtue."[25] What men failed to see was that Beecher and women like her everywhere were gaining power by indirection in assuming not only the duties of home and child rearing, but in maintaining the arts and other cultural activities as well. Ironically, men's eagerness to relegate what they felt were nonessential, even unmasculine, tasks to women eventually provided females with broad contacts in the culture and helped to lodge them as a pervasive influence in society. Beecher's work in preparing women for teaching and placing them in schools throughout the country was, intentional or not, a major step in that direction and while her endorsement of lower wages for female teachers may have run against the grain in one sense, it demonstrated her contention that women were well suited to making personal sacrifices for the sake of the culture. "Catharine Beecher not only wanted to 'save' the nation, she wanted women to save it," and as she herself put it, teaching "is a *profession*, offering influence, respectability and independence," because, as she noted in 1835, "it is chimerical to hope" for male teachers "when there are multitudes of other employments that will...lead to wealth."[26]

The American male diverted or sublimated his energy away from the house (and thus the women in it) to a world of limitless opportunities and because much of that energy was sexual, by channeling it as he did he was testing his masculinity against the challenges of nature and business. As shown earlier, Tocqueville eliminated from the American male psychology the natural attraction to women and nature, and later he refines this point even further: "The American republics of the present day are like companies of adventurers, formed to explore in common the waste lands of the New World, and busied in a flourishing trade. The passions which agitate the Americans most deeply, are not their political, but their commercial passions; or, to speak more correctly, they introduce the habits they contract in business into their political life."[27] This passionate involvement in commerce and expansion required men undistracted by women, yet such a manly world was morally risky and chaotic, making order (both moral and literal) in the home an absolute necessity if the nation was to progress without collapsing. With convoluted logic, the male claimed that woman was the mainstay of a good and orderly society precisely because she remained apart from society and without heterosexual desires that could only reduce a man's energetic pursuit of success.

If woman represented morality and order, she also represented civilization in the sense of a restrictive influence and unmanly refinement. Given those responsibilities men disdained for themselves—morals, children, domestic routine, the arts, and manners—she was kept busy and contained, but she also possessed considerable power in her assigned role because of these responsibilities, power that, if left unchecked or submitted to through continual contact, would hamper the male in his efforts for gain, his passion for commerce. Civilization, like genuine heterosexuality, threatened male autonomy, something the rugged individual could not stand for, and so he fled, either from home to business or from East to West. Or both, if pioneers can be seen as entrepreneurs, a view recalling Tocqueville's description above of Americans as "companies of adventurers, formed to explore in common the waste lands of the New World." Thus, westward expansion was characterized not only by a flight of anxious males but by what Fiedler has called "the holy marriage of males," a "homoerotic" or latent homosexual union between them.[28] The West represented undefiled democracy, an unfeminized and, therefore, uncivilized, nondomesticated equality that men could exercise in pursuit of wealth and autonomy. It was their last, best hope. Yet the gaining of wealth and the assertion of autonomy had to be accomplished at the expense of someone or something, and this presents an apparent contradiction in the nineteenth-century male psychology.

Earlier it was maintained that the American male inherited a recurrent, unconscious distrust of woman associated with hostile nature—a mythological construct traceable through Protestant thought to the Garden of Eden where Adam, unwilling to act against Eve and the forces of evil embodied in nature, yielded and was lost. Yet it has also been stated that, paradoxically, woman came to be associated with civilization—the opposite of nature—in the male mind. Both concepts are possible, however, because that mind, consciously or not, was capable of rendering them compatible. For men to define and to assert their masculinity, they had to seek its opposite so that it could be rejected or avoided as inferior. This meant, of course, women or, more precisely, femininity and because women were identified with civilization as a means of containing and neutralizing them, men could see only too well where the threat to their masculinity lay. In fleeing that threat, they gave form to the other concept with female nature the object of their sublimated energy and the rape of the virgin forests and land the metaphorical equivalent of a historical fact: a reenactment of Adamic resentment over that fateful moment in the Garden, a drama made possible by a new land and a culture that set the democratic scene and provided the technological props.[29]

In the classic literature of the nineteenth century, the West, as a second Eden in which the masculine alliance—again, Fiedler's holy marriage of males—played out its hostility toward women and female nature, was not always a West of endless plains, sagebrush, or forested mountains but was, instead, often portrayed as a "raft floating down the river, an isolated valley on a South Sea island, a lonely wood sought as a refuge from combat, a ship on the open sea. What it cannot be is city or village, hearth or home; for isolation is the key, the non-presence of the customary."[30] And it was here, in a new Eden beyond the society men have fled ever since Rip Van Winkle and Natty Bumppo, that the American male imagination sought sufficient relief and revenge to be reborn a second Adam, one capable of adding a new and important chapter to his mythological past. The epic waters in the works of Poe, Melville, and Twain baptize their boyish characters into the world of experience, a world of men pitted against each other and nature in terror-ridden battles for survival and supremacy, a world without women from which boys return, washed of their innocence, as men ready to tell their manly tales. Yet they remain boys forever because they have sought their masculine freedom—at root a psychosexual concept of self—not in the brothel, the bedroom, or the genuinely heterosexual marriage, but in the company of other males.

Richard Henry Dana's *Two Years before the Mast* is yet another example of this phenomenon, and Wright Morris's essay in the 1964 edition reveals how ingrained the rite of passage is in the American mind. In fact, Morris's comments pertain not just to Dana's novel but to all such watery Westerns in which nature provides both the setting and the adversary for stories of young, wandering men:

> Although Dana describes life on board simply and clearly, certain details, of interest to the modern reader, go unmentioned. Neither his temperament, nor the times, were appropriate. The life of men without women would receive a different emphasis today. It is the very absence of this emphasis, on which the modern reader is sated, that gives to this report, strange as it should seem, a manliness and a sanity that the sex-ridden adventure curiously lacks, where men are too often reduced to the state of sick animals. Seeing how much can be said without it, would many modern readers wish it inserted? I doubt it. It is one of the obsessions that the modern mind seeks to escape. In Dana's civilized, well-bred mind, a concept of what a *man* is is always present; this unspoken assurance gives the book its character. Boys soon to be men have long found in it much food for thought. If masts are not so high as they once seemed, the sea still takes and gives a man's measure, and the depth of the sea may prove to be more profound than space. From it life once emerged, and if necessary it will emerge again.[31]

The wilderness of water is the source of life, the supreme test of maleness, and Morris finds in Dana's tale (and, by implication, others like it) relief from the world of women, sex, and the insanity inherent in heterosexual complications. The pure male must seek, if not literally then imaginatively through literature, the company of men who are both dependent on and in conflict with a nature at once the source of life and the harbinger of destruction. Men used the very things they despised the most— the literal and figurative female—the one to propel them in an opposite direction, the other to give them an adversary they could defeat, or at least try to. In thereby avenging himself on his civilization and mythical past, the American male was, in R.W.B. Lewis's words, "a new Adam, miraculously free of family and race, untouched by those dismal conditions which prior tragedies and entanglements monotonously prepared for the newborn European."[32] This second Adam was free to remain in the Garden of the New World and to redefine it for his own purposes, allowing others—such as the original inhabitants, the Indians—to remain only under specified conditions of inferiority and finding justification from fellow members of the masculine alliance.

Support for male dominance came from several sources including some not directly linked to the West, and one of the most persuasive was the medical profession since in the nineteenth century (as in the twentieth) the doctor was a leading figure in the culture, a man whose opinions counted and who received respect bordering on awe. He was visible proof that hard work and diligence paid off, but more important still he was the successful man who combined two of society's cherished ideals: the superiority of applied science and technology over pure science as agents of progress; and the businessman *par excellence* whose ready-made, dependent clientele guaranteed his prosperity. Furthermore, medical men in general had as much at stake in preserving the values of the culture as the people had in them for preserving their health, and thus doctors were some of the most distinguished members of the masculinity cult, the American Medical Association (AMA) a bastion of conservative ideology, and together they provided an authoritative stamp of approval on the concept of male superiority.

The practice of medicine—allied as it was to higher education, technology, and business—naturally had to be put in the hands of men. Moreover, in the first years of the nineteenth century, states began requiring attendance at a medical school and examinations as prerequisites for licensing, and by the late 1820s all but three states had enacted laws controlling the practice of medicine, which automatically excluded women. Within a decade, female practitioners whose only training had been the trial and error of firsthand experiences had all but disappeared. This upgrading process involving institutionalization and legal regulation was normal not just for medicine but for other sciences as well, and the inevitable elimination of women as a side effect paralleled what had happened in medicine in sixteenth-century Europe. Generally speaking, the advantages of the process for patients and physicians alike cannot be denied, yet it is also true that progress for one or more groups of people is often gained at the expense of another: "Women were," as one historian has written, "the casualties of medical professionalization."[33]

Sanctions against female physicians remained strong for most of the century and constituted the medical profession's version of the male manifesto.[34] Doctors, no less than other men, saw danger in female places and reacted accordingly, spurred as they were by such events as the first Women's Rights Convention at Seneca Falls in 1848, the passage in many states of married women's property acts by 1850, and the fledgling suffrage movement led by Elizabeth Cady Stanton and Susan B. Anthony. The Civil War supplied a graphic, if crude, distinction between the sexes that further encouraged men in their maleness since they, not women, had fought to retain the Union, and it could then be argued that the union of men had to be retained as well.

Concerning medicine in particular, professionalization took form in an attack against midwifery (a lay occupation that avoided the usual obstacles to getting a medical license) and gave rise to gynecology as a specialty for male doctors, many of whom were general practitioners and obstetricians who saw an opportunity to improve their lot and at the same time express their views about women. Augustus Kinsley Gardner, an obstetrician turned gynecologist, implied a general disgust for women in his scoffing remarks about political activists, those who wore bloomers, and midwives: "At the present time [1852] there is a proposition mooted—springing from the same high source which advocates womans rights, the Bloomer costume, and other similar nonsensical theories—to give again the portion of the healing art, if not the whole domain of medicine, to the females."[35] The "portion of the healing art" Gardner refers to is midwifery, and his remarks betray the anxiety he shared with other physicians who, in keeping with the age, attacked women as a means of protecting themselves.

The advent of gynecology was part of what Donald B. Meyer has called "a special pathology, not the disciplined, long-practised style, but a defensive, emergency ideology....Men had their own passion, and at the prospect of emancipated women recoiled with that fright special to those addicted to an obsession."[36] This fear of women was expressed by Alfred Stille, president of the AMA, who, in 1871, declared that some women "seek to rival men in manly sports and occupations, and the 'strong-minded' ape them assiduously in all things, even in dress. In doing so, they may command a sort of admiration such as all monstrous productions acquire, especially when they tend toward a higher type than their own."[37] Stille's belief that men should be regarded as a "higher type" than women and that any female aspirations to the contrary were "monstrous" was representative of his profession and his time vis-à-vis the rise of social Darwinism after the Civil War: an elaborate rationalization for paternalism to keep women in a childlike state of innocence and thereby render them ineffective in the male world. According to one writer at mid-century, "True feminine genius is ever timid, doubtful, and clingingly dependent; a perpetual childhood," and an advice book for young ladies prescribed that women should "become as little children" and "avoid a controversial spirit."[38]

Because nineteenth-century men were uneasy about heterosexual involvement as female entrapment, it seems inevitable in retrospect that physicians, as male authority figures for the culture, would have expressed that fear most graphically since they, unlike other men, had direct and legal access to women's bodies. The history of gynecology is, therefore, in part the history of male tyranny over women who had nowhere else to turn for medical treatment once the midwife had been discredited. The founder of gynecology, J. Marion Sims, established himself as an expert on the subject, thus setting many of the precedents his profession would follow. Sims, a man who feared competition almost as much as failure, referred to the surgical knife as a "weapon," suggesting that he would accomplish his gynecological feats not in spite of but because of the fact that, in his own words, "if there was anything I hated, it was investigating the organs of the female pelvis."[39]

Sims thus destroyed or mutilated those organs whenever he could during the decades following his first surgery in 1845, and he stands as an extreme example of a widespread male belief that it was in women's best interest (and, therefore, society's) to be circumscribed with dependence, children, domestic cares, and a harmless morality and sexuality. This concern for keeping them in their place was intensified after the Civil War when emancipated blacks and immigrants joined restless women in the male mind to heighten his anxiety over possible cultural displacement. Women, blacks, and immigrants were, after all, seen by the WASP male as essentially the same: intellectually and socially inferior but sexually potent and, therefore, threatening. Rebelliousness in women was not, of course, limited to the political and economic demands of the suffragists and those who aspired to professional careers although these constituted obvious challenges to male autonomy that, because of their visibility, had to be countered in ways that would make male resistance appear benevolent. David M. Kennedy claims that such benevolence kept women not just psychologically weak but physically impaired as well:

> The pathologic effects of the regimen of sheltered domesticity were not all psychological. The helplessness of the American woman—especially in the urban East and the upper-class South—owed at least as much to real physiological weakness as it did to compliance with a rigid moral ideal.... Robert Latou Dickinson insisted in the 1890s that the neurasthenic female was more than a caricature and that the causes of her condition were plain: lack of exercise and ridiculous standards of dress.... The rigid "health waists" were especially damaging to working girls who leaned forward all day over a typewriter or a sewing machine. Still, in spite of almost daily evidence of the injury done to women by overdomestication and overdressing, the American male—whose house women kept and for whose eye they attired themselves—

continued to pride himself on the manly protection he offered his delicate, dependent charges.[40]

Men argued against political and economic reform for women in terms of what was best for the home, society, orderly progress, and women themselves, the last point being the paternalistic *coup de grace* suggesting that women, by their very nature, were disruptive not only of a male society but of their own proper sphere as well. Female modesty and an orderly society were linked as cause and effect, and the maintenance of this relationship required submission to the male manifesto. And just as blacks often tried to subvert or escape political, social, and geographic constraints—usually in vain—women often sought at least a temporary stay against cultural prejudice and the psychosexual problems it caused. To this end, countless women patronized various health centers devoted to curing female problems. Between the 1840s and the 1880s, over two hundred watercure clinics were established, and respected authorities such as Catharine Beecher encouraged women to visit them because they offered services unavailable anywhere else in America, including the standard medical fields: "There female communality replaced the characteristic isolation of American domestic life, bodily sensuality could be freely indulged, and an unwanted pregnancy might even be terminated. Most importantly, at a time when orthodox medicine offered women little more than biblical admonitions on the inevitability of pain, hydropathy sympathetically sought to meliorate the wide variety of ailments and diseases associated with female reproductive processes."[41]

Culturally approved health centers for middle and upper class women were places they could turn to—or be sent to by their vexed husbands—for relief from and rejuvenation in a male-oriented society, which, medically, tended to dismiss female hysteria, depression, and diseases of the reproductive organs as nothing more than typical problems of the weaker sex. And because women were, according to Sklar, "no longer willing to take a heavenly reward instead of a worldly cure, they were born a generation too late to be mollified by Roxana Beecher's attitude of religious resignation, but too early to benefit from the medical advances—especially germ theory—that trans-

formed gynecological medicine at the end of the nineteenth century."[42] In particular, puerperal fever, a massive killer of women
in childbirth, was fairly well understood by the latter decades
of the nineteenth century; yet gynecologists were reluctant to
treat the disease by means of antisepsis, and through the 1870s,
1880s, and 1890s most obstetrical surgeons ignored Lister's discovery in the 1860s of the bacterial causes of infection. As Sklar
has stated it, "the period of 'Victorianism' coincides with the
period when women were conscious of the hazards connected
with their physiology, were unwilling to die because of them,
but were as yet unable to obtain effective medical cures."[43] If
women who visited health "retreats"—an especially significant
term in this context—could not be assured of lasting relief from
physical and psychological ailments, they could at least gain
sympathy and attention from other women plus a temporary
respite from the role their culture expected them to fill. In this
regard, spas and other rehabilitation centers for women were
the female equivalent of the masculine alliance, both sexes separating themselves from each other to circumvent culturally in-
duced, psychosexual tensions.

   In her study of the causes, treatment, and cultural implications
of female hysteria in nineteenth-century America, Carrol Smith-
Rosenberg cites conflicting role expectations as a significant part
of the problem:

> The American girl was taught at home, at school, and in the
> literature of the period, that aggression, independence, self-as-
> sertion and curiosity were male traits, inappropriate for the weaker
> sex and her limited sphere. Dependent throughout her life, she
> was to reward her male protectors with affection and submission.
> At no time was she expected to achieve in any area considered
> important by men and thus highly valued by society. She was,
> in essence, to remain a child-woman, never developing the
> strengths and skills of adult autonomy.[44]

This cultural conditioning of girls to create ideal women eventually conflicted with the actual world they inhabited where
another ideal, that of motherhood, took over. Now, instead of
being weak and delicate, she was expected to be protective and
efficient in terms of the family and the home, to carry out a

variety of tasks without complaint, and to face the extreme physical pain and high death rate of childbirth: all this while remaining submissive to males whom the culture had declared
stronger. As the neurologist S. Weir Mitchell wrote in 1887, "We
may be sure that our daughters will be more likely to have to
face at some time the grim question of pain than the lads who
grow up beside them," even though boys were taught to accept
pain without a whimper while girls were expected to respond
with tears and the need for sympathy.[45]

The result of this confusion of sex roles and the tension created
between the ideal woman versus the ideal mother was often
some form of hysteria as an unconscious expression of unhap-
piness and disorientation. Yet because even adult women were
considered by men to be childlike in their dependence on them,
hysteria was just as often diagnosed as a reversion to childish
unruliness and rebellion and should, therefore, be treated accordingly. This placed physicians in the difficult position of attempting to treat a child and a woman in the same person—not
to mention the wife of another man—and as Smith-Rosenberg
has stated, "In a number of cases...the physician...played the
role of oedipal father figure to the patient's child-woman role,
and in such instances his complicity was not only moral and
intellectual but sexual as well. These doctors had become part
of a domestic triangle—a husband's rival, the fatherly attendant
of a daughter."[46] Both to protect themselves and to treat the
patient according to prevailing cultural and medical assumptions, doctors exerted their authority—patriarchal as well as
professional—over the female adult-child:

> Much of the treatment prescribed by physicians for hysteria re-
> flects, in its draconic severity, their need to exert control—and,
> when thwarted, their impulse to punish. Doctors frequently rec-
> ommended suffocating hysterical women until their fits stopped,
> beating them across the face and body with wet towels, ridiculing
> and exposing them in front of family and friends, showering them
> with icy water. "The mode adopted to arrest this curious malady,"
> a physician connected with a large mental hospital wrote, "con-
> sists in making some strong and sudden impression on the mind
> through...the most potent of all impressions, fear....Ridicule to
> a woman of sensitive mind, is a powerful weapon...but there is

no emotion equal to fear and the threat of personal chastise-
ment....They will listen to the voice of authority."[47]

And in another related vein, John Demos states that "recent
research on the history of gynecology has uncovered a demand,
in an astonishing number of cases, for the surgical procedure of
clitoridectomy. Evidently this was the last resort of women who,
contrary to expectation, found themselves afflicted with 'sensual' wishes."[48]

The point to be made here is the woman's submission to the
masculine imperative and the relief medical science granted her
from having to deal consciously with heterosexuality, an act of
darkness she was obliged by cultural and religious mandate to
regard as woman's fate, however bothersome or disgusting. Furthermore, the male's authority and virility were demonstrated
in the active versus passive role: an extreme yet representative
reenactment on the most literal sexual level of the mythological
assault on the frontier, on female nature, by men holding a
repressed Edenic grudge and having something to prove.

Masculine energy ravaged the land even as it dominated the
female mind and body, and male righteousness in both cases
was not to be compromised once J. Marion Sims—and many of
his colleagues by association—acting like a Daniel Boone gone
beserk over the riches to be gained from new territory, had
opened and explored the womb, shaped and carved the genitals,
and found the technology to make intimidating women submit.
The analogy of Sims and the pioneer-frontiersman recalls what
Fiedler has written about Natty Bumppo, and it helps to illuminate the comparison:

> He is overtly pious, meek, chaste (of course!), sententious—often
> a bore, a Protestant Noble Savage, worshipping in the Universalist
> Church of the Woods; and yet he is also a dangerous symbol of
> Cooper's secret protest against the gentle tyranny of home and
> woman. A white man, who knows the "gifts" of his color and
> will not take a scalp or be rude to a lady, a man without caste,
> who knows his place and recognizes all officers and gentlemen
> as his superiors, his is still a law unto himself: judge and exe-
> cutioner, the man with the gun, the killer—however reluctant.
> He is the prototype of all pioneers, trappers, cowboys, and other

innocently destructive children of nature, which is to say, of the Westerner, quick on the draw and immune to guilt.[49]

In nineteenth-century America, the womb and the land were one, and men—Old Testament patriarchs whose time had come at last—fought unconsciously against both that they might never be children again.

The nineteenth century valued science not only for the technology it made possible but also for the data and learned opinions it supplied in support of popular ideology. Various branches of science and the social sciences extended Aristotle's hierarchy of superior-inferior forms and the eighteenth-century concept of the Chain of Being to classify both the races and the sexes according to natural abilities:

> Since at least the time of Hippocrates and Aristotle, the roles assigned women have attracted an elaborate body of medical and biological justifications. This was especially true in the nineteenth century as the intellectual and emotional centrality of science increased steadily. Would-be scientific arguments were used in the rationalization and legitimization of almost every aspect of Victorian life, and with particular vehemence in those areas in which social change implied stress in existing social arrangements.[50]

As might be expected, Caucasians were found racially superior and females were found inferior to males. In 1878, Paul Topinard, an anthropologist, published a summary of scientific opinions indicating that these conclusions were valid beyond doubt, based as they were on the skull capacities of various races and the sexes.[51] Encouraged by science and the sociological Darwinism of Herbert Spencer, American males could stratify the culture with themselves at the top and, in the process, condescend to women for much the same reasons that they looked down upon racial and ethnic minorities, particularly the blacks. In their study of medical views of sexuality in Victorian America, John and Robin Haller state that "with arguments weighted by the value-laden statistics of medical science, society skirted the coarseness of contemporary racial language by constructing a shallow paternalism that not only placed woman under constant

medical guardianship but also recast contemporary racial terminology to demonstrate her innate inferiority to the male."[52]

Popular medical opinion held woman to be both the result
and victim of her reproductive system, her biological woman-
ness, and doctors reasoned that her cultural role was thus defined—wife and mother—and her capricious, oftentimes
hysterical, behavior was an inevitable aspect of her nature.[53]
Men, on the other hand, were declared by male physicians to
be far less susceptible to control by their reproductive systems.
As Charles D. Meigs, a well-known Philadelphia gynecologist,
wrote in 1847, woman is "a moral, a sexual, a germiferous,
gestative and parturient creature."[54] And regarding woman's
biologically determined social role, a physician remarked in 1882
that it was as if "the Almighty, in creating the female sex, had
taken the uterus and built up a woman around it."[55] The implication here is that equivalents to these female traits do not
exist in the male, at least not to the extent that moral, sexual,
reproductive, and familial urges could control his destiny.

Their intellectual capacity limited by a smaller brain and their
bodies subject to menstrual reminders of their biological destiny,
women were compelled to finish their schooling early and marry
soon afterward for the sake of the race since, according to one
physician, college and remaining single made "wifehood and
motherhood distasteful owing to defective development of the
sexual organs," and any woman who accepted her biological
duty must also accept the fact that the responsibilities of motherhood were "direct rivals of brain work, for they both require
for their performance an exclusive and plentiful supply of phos-
phates."[56] In other words, both brain work and biological work
were impossible in the female, and emphasis on one could only
be detrimental to the other with potentially dire consequences
not just for the woman but for her children and even the race.

This concern over the apparent deterioration of American
women—especially those of the middle and upper class—heightened in the last decades of the century as men recalled the
sturdiness of their pioneering mothers and grandmothers and
contrasted with alarm the condition of their own wives to the
hardiness and durability of immigrant females. Many physicians
and educators believed that too much education during the bi-

ologically crucial years of puberty and adolescence caused underdeveloped reproductive systems that would, in turn, produce puny offspring. The female body was viewed as a limited system with a limited supply of energy and if, therefore, a young woman diverted that energy to intellectual matters, the body would be robbed of the vital forces required to develop its reproductive abilities. As one study of this attitude describes it, "the brain and ovary could not develop at the same time," and "all the doyens of American gynecology in the late-nineteenth century—Emmett, J. Marion Sims, T. Gaillard Thomas, Charles D. Meigs, William Goodell, and Mitchell—shared the conviction that higher education and excessive development of the nervous system might interfere with woman's proper performance of her maternal functions."[57] Thus, even those institutions of higher learning that admitted women often reflected a concern for keeping priorities straight by giving female students reduced academic loads or even barring them from regular degree programs. According to the regents of the University of Wisconsin in 1877, "every physiologist is well aware that at stated times, nature makes a great demand upon the energies of early womanhood and that at these times great caution must be exercised lest injury be done. . . . Education is greatly to be desired, but it is better that the future matrons of the state should be robust, hearty, healthy women, than that, by over study, they entail upon their descendants the germs of disease."[58]

Oddly enough, in voicing their distress over the physical deterioration of American women, men were reacting to a real problem although their analyses of that problem were misguided since its origins were cultural and not tied to some relationship between intellectual and physiological development. That is, in the last decades of the nineteenth century, many middle class and most upper class women were required to conform to the genteel tradition of restrictive clothing, "feminine" interests, and idleness as a status symbol. These, of course, had deleterious effects on women, and their men were understandably concerned.

In reacting the way they did, however, many of the influential men failed to recognize that it was the male-oriented culture that had helped to produce such women; instead they supported solutions revealing unconscious fears for their own well being. If women were allowed to receive as much training as men, it follows that they would hope to use that training and thereby compete with men, a trend which would displace the male in the working world and disrupt domestic harmony. Furthermore, in citing the vigor of uneducated immigrant women and placing the responsibility for future generations of healthy Anglo-Saxon children on mothers who should, for the sake of the race, be similarly uneducated, WASP males were expressing their anxiety over cultural rather than just occupational displacement. Robust immigrant sons would outstrip and overwhelm sickly American sons unless their mothers and future mothers remained at home, allowing their maternal bodies rather than their human minds to mature. "We want," one authority declared, "to have body as well as mind, otherwise the degeneration of the race is inevitable," and Smith-Rosenberg and Rosenberg have commented on this attitude that "such transcendent responsibilities made the individual woman's personal ambitions seem trivial indeed."[59] And it was Herbert Spencer's contention that the female's physical evolution had stopped long before the male's in order to retain her strong, almost animalistic, abilities to reproduce, and that the mothering instinct had, in turn, provided her with certain psychological and emotional traits enabling her to survive against more powerful, aggressive males. Such qualities as love, pity, intuition, and passivity were, however, no longer necessary for literal survival in the nineteenth century, and thus they were best applied in the home where altruism and sentimentality, contained in their proper sphere, would not impede male work and society's progress. This was, Spencer claimed, the natural order of things: "Reverencing power more than men do, women respected freedom less," and true women would, therefore, yield to male authority without a sense of loss because individual freedom was not so important as mankind's evolutionary mission.[60]

Besides Spencer's profound misjudgment of which sex worshipped power in the nineteenth century—the correct assessment was Tocqueville's much earlier—the English sociologist corroborated a popular misconception by separating female sexuality and psychology, the one active, the other passive, and channeling each to meet his own ideological ends without having to consider the total personality. To recognize and account for that personality, a snarl of psychosexual and cultural forces, could only have complicated the Spencerian penchant for the unemcumbered advancement of a male-dominated society. Those who objected to the notion of men's physical and mental superiority were countered by Spencerians who claimed that the entire history of women's behavior demonstrated "overwhelming external evidence of the existence of such differences."[61] These differences were attributed in large part to the struggle for survival among the fittest, which had equipped the male so well that he would continue to excel over the female—a point of curcuitous logic that said men were fittest to struggle, and the struggle made them fittest. Women were thus excluded from the competition by virtue of being women, and their chances of ever entering the fray at all, let alone as equals, were slim:

> Spencerians asserted that the laws of heredity, although imperfectly understood, had increased the mental endowment of the male at an almost geometric proportion over that of the female. Drawing from Darwin's law of transmission and from Spencer's inverse ratio between individuation and multiplication, they argued that not only would the intellectual mother have fewer daughters than the average mother, but also that "the chances of transmission of intellectual qualities in the female line will be lessened as culture increases among mothers."[62]

In her study of Catharine Beecher and the culture she lived in, Kathryn Kish Sklar has observed that "as the potential options open to women in the nineteenth century became further clarified in the third decade, Catharine generally participated in the bargain then being struck between women's social role and domesticity. If women would agree to limit their participation in the society as a whole, so the pact has been described, then they could ascend to total hegemony over the domestic sphere."[63] And, like Beecher, Sarah Hale—widowed mother and editor of *Godey's Lady's Book*—believed that women could achieve positive ends for themselves and society through moderation rather than militancy. Destined to be the agent of culture and moral insight because men had neither the time nor the inclination for these tasks, women should provide balance to a culture otherwise tipped too far in the pursuit of wealth, and the future of America, Hale maintained, was thus in the hands of wives, mothers, and professional women who did not directly challenge male prerogatives in the world outside the home. As she said of women, "there is for them but *one* pursuit. Of what use is it for us to deny the fact, that it is in the marriage establishment only, that woman seeks her happiness and expects her importance, when all history and our own observation, confirm it to be the truth. It is not so with men—they have more than *one* medium through which to seek for fortune, fame and happiness, and that is, in my opinion, the sole reason of their superiority of mind over us."[64]

Given the fact, however, that Hale recognized why men had more opportunities—because they were men—and, in addition, that she was a mother who never remarried after the early death of her husband, it is likely that her statements on marriage as woman's greatest hope were at least partially intended to keep men off balance. As one historian has put it, "Beneath the soft exterior of motherhood and femininity Sarah Hale was a shrewd and businesslike woman whose...dealings with male contributors to Godey's proved her more than a match for the...entrepreneurs who were making their way in literature. Though she may have preferred to knit rather than to whittle, she could bargain with the best of them."[65]

Other than the followers of straightforward feminists such as Elizabeth Cady Stanton and Angelina and Sarah Grimke, most men and women opted for Beecher and Hale's cultural *quid pro quo*—Fiedler and Trecker's "Faustian bargain"—which was not only more moderate but more subtle, too. Men were not yet capable of accepting blunt efforts for full equality for women based on the eighteenth-century doctrine of natural rights, but they were more than willing to give women the home, the schoolroom, and the local arts society since doing so kept them out of the male domain while providing a measure of stability to a society in constant flux. Beecher, for instance, saw antebellum America as filled with agitation and anxiety—e.g., westward expansion and the slavery issue—and she thus contended that if women kept their proper places, using them to the fullest, antagonism could be held within bearable limits.[66]

Beecher's ideology of domesticity granted women a particular and important function, yet the importance was relative and compared to the power and status white males enjoyed during the first decades of the century, it fell further and further behind. Men and economic production were leaving the home at an increasing rate and, as Sklar explains, "much of Catharine Beecher's life work can be seen as a bridge across the growing gap that separated the rising expectations of early nineteenth-century women from the social, political, and economic realities of their culture," realities that suggest that a doctrine of self-sacrifice was as much a recognition of male domination as it was an alternative to it:

> The dependency roles to which women were increasingly reduced in the nineteenth century had a direct and deleterious effect on their own sense of self. . . . An ideology of self-sacrifice could mask some of the losses women felt about their status in the first half of the nineteenth century, but it supplied inadequate nourishment for their crippled sense of self-esteem. Along with an absolute loss of economic status, and a relative loss of political status, women also experienced an absolute loss of personal autonomy during the middle decades of the nineteenth century. Recent scholarship . . . has measured the extent to which the personal identities of women were attached to the family into which they were born in the eighteenth century but were cut off from that root in the nineteenth century and more completely appended to their husbands. . . . In the minds of many, dependency was the natural state of womanhood and to throw off these ties was to commit an antisocial and unnatural act. . . . Catharine Beecher was not the only woman who paid homage to the cult of "true womanhood" but regularly broke out of its constraints.[67]

Science, medicine, and social theory were brought to bear on women in the last century to accentuate and to protect the WASP male's sense of his own superiority as well as to discourage competition in the working world where men proved, or attempted to prove, their masculinity. As suggested earlier, this elitism was not only sexual but racial, and women, therefore, were accorded an inferior status similar to that of blacks who had found that slavery could take other forms after emancipation:

> In their studies of the Victorian woman, Spencerians paid obsequious attendance to those psychological and anthropometric peculiarities which seemed to relate her to the "inferior races." They saw in woman's physical and mental characteristics a remarkable resemblance to the Negro in the nineteenth-century evolutionary framework, and their conclusions, like those regarding the politics of southern reconstruction, tended to project a similar foreboding to any change in the woman's station in life. . . . They viewed any effort which ignored woman's "natural" station as a reckless attempt to flout the laws of nature—an attempt which carried women beyond the pale of femininity and drove them relentlessly back to a more diseased and atavistic stage of sex development.[68]

This belief in sexual and racial classification—the male WASP ego—was given blunt expression by William K. Brooks, a zoology professor at Johns Hopkins University, when he wrote that "the positions which women already occupy in society and the duties which they perform are, in the main, what they should be if our view of them is correct; and any attempt to improve the condition of women by ignoring or obliterating the intellectual differences between them and men must result in disaster to the race, and the obstruction of that progress and improvement which the history of the past shows to be in store for both men and women in the future."[69]

With women's intellectual inferiority to men established by the authoritative voice of a Spencerian academic, medical doctors trained by men such as Brooks could cinch the analogy between women and blacks. Such was the message from the physician George F. Talbot who lamented that America's "heroic effort" had freed a million ignorant slaves, given them "the rank of citizens and electors," and resulted in "negro members of Congress," a situation that moved him to wonder "if the effect of raising to the grade of voters the whole mass of illiterate slaves was to give them the whole political control of several States, why will not this complete enfranchisement of women give them the political control in all the older States, where they will be in the numerical majority."[70] Women were to be denied the vote—symbol of freedom and equality in a democracy—because, like blacks, they threatened white male autonomy and the power structure it required for the unrestricted release of masculine energy.

Furthermore, if blacks were granted political and economic equality, by implication they would gain sexual equality, too, and this would have meant the horrifying prospect of equal access to white women for males known to be racially inferior but reputed to be sexually potent: the final assault on the white man's domain by blacks and women united against him. Thus, their development was retarded by men who sought masculine security by keeping others in an infantile, nonheterosexual state of innocence, ostensibly to protect them from a world they were ill equipped to comprehend but actually to protect that world, in all its maleness, from nonwhite, nonmale claims to power. Carl Degler maintains that because women had so much in common with blacks, they "learned to accommodate themselves to those with power—that is men—so that they cajoled rather than demanded, just as Negroes would play 'dumb' or shuffle foolishly because that kind of deferential behavior was what white men wanted and responded positively to.... Women, like Negroes, are highly visible socially so that prejudice against them is immediately triggered and cannot be assuaged or eliminated by covert association and familiarity, as might occur with a Jew or a Catholic. Thus for women, as for Negroes, discrimination has been more tenacious and pervasive than for other minorities."[71]

Elsewhere, Degler has stated his resistance to the claim "that women were generally seen in the nineteenth century as without sexual feelings or drives," and his call for a more balanced view is reasonable insofar as there were numerous medical and moral authorities who insisted that women did possess sexual desire.[72] But Degler misses the point, or rather does not take his far enough, since the central issue does not involve the existence of female sexuality *per se*—obviously it existed or there would not have been such concern—but the male's fear of that sexuality as a potential source of power. Female sexuality had to be suppressed to assure male superiority because sex meant energy and power, and urban men had to subdue women just as the pioneer had to conquer the virgin land. If, as Degler himself has said, blacks and women occupied similar positions in the male WASP mind, then a sexual threat from one would suggest at least a potential sexual threat from the other, though they clearly took different forms. Degler concedes that, given the Victorian view of sexuality, "there was an effort to deny women's sexual feelings and to deny them legitimate expression," but counters that concession by claiming that "the many writings by medical men who spoke in a contrary vein...should make us doubt that the ideology was actually put into practice by most men or women of the nineteenth century, even among the middle class, though it was to this class in particular that the admonitions and ideology were directed."[73] This may be true although there was sufficient male action against female sexuality—both literal and symbolic—to cast doubt on Degler's conclusion. But regardless of Degler's thesis that the ideology was not acted upon by the majority of males, it remains just that, an ideology, which indicates a pervasive set of attitudes held by men who may not have always been able to enforce in practice what they pursued in belief but who believed nonetheless: women and blacks were sexual threats to the masculinity cult, and male attitudes responded accordingly. Finally, it can be argued that those medical men who spoke on behalf of women were not so much a part of their time as ahead of it, given the profession's general reluctance—and gynecologists' in particular—to employ the latest findings concerning infection and the inhumane treatments frequently prescribed for female disorders.

One response for men was to convert women into something more congenial to the male ego, and they often became, as one writer put it, "nature's nuns" who constituted a "race of physically passive and of mentally neutralized women" and who should, therefore, be content in their bland purity, a view upheld and enforced by various medical men as high priests of the culture.[74] The Hallers' description of the medical opinion of woman as a "noncompetitive helpmate" recalls Tocqueville's observation above that the husband sees his wife as nothing more than "a detached portion of himself":

> Concealing their punitive moralism in the guise of medical prog-

nosis, doctors maintained the facade of the disinterested professional when faced with the open discontent of the woman seeking
to fulfill her potentialities as a human being. Having identified
her as a "lesser man," they could only accept a passive, self-
denigrating, and noncompetitive helpmate. Any effort on her part
to deny or escape that role was considered an unnatural atavism
that only reaffirmed her dependent and parasitic nature. Woman's efforts to escape from the home circle merely precipitated
any number of newer medical theories to explain her actions.[75]

Physicians no less than ministers were the moral authorities
in nineteenth-century America, and in many ways their pro-
nouncements were more influential than those from the pulpit
since physicians treated all women, not just believers, with their
pseudo-secularism and their conclusions were backed by science
rather than faith. While scientists and doctors purported to use
the latest, most sophisticated methods of objective inquiry to
study women, they in fact were society's moral agents whose
primary goal was, as Trecker has pointed out, to wedge females
into various "biological, evolutionary, and anthropological
theories":

> Most of these hypotheses were characterized by a dualistic bias
> which saw the female in all ways as the complement and contrary
> of the male. This prescientific habit of mind, combined with a
> belief in the objectivity of research and the purity of scientific
> study, permitted conservative 19th century doctors, scientists and
> educators to rework earlier theories about women's rights and
> place, without realizing that the origin of their ideas lay not in
> their empirical data, but in their cultural heritage. . . . They mea-
> sured skulls, weighed brains, charted aptitudes for mathematics
> and tested memory; they figured out the average male consump-
> tion of food and studied the lives of individuals of genius. When
> they finished and made their recommendations for the proper
> role and education of women, however, they spoke with St. Paul
> and Rousseau about the complementary physical and psycholog-
> ical nature of the sexes and the subordination of women.[76]

Traveling different roads in their search for definitive answers
to woman's proper and symbolic role, physicians and ministers
eventually arrived at the same point, and together they were a

persuasive, harmonious voice speaking to the culture. The male manifesto thus reached deep into American life through one or both of these agents: a combination of secular guilt and Old Testament resentment leaving women their homes and children to care for as penitent outcasts from the paranoid, asexual world of men. David Kennedy states that "men saw themselves as patriarchal and authoritarian because they suppressed a sexual nature that was aggressive, even potentially brutal. And they saw woman as innocent, dependent, good, and generous because she was—ideally—sexless," and the physician William Acton declared that "many of the best mothers, wives and managers of households know little of or are careless about sexual indulgences. Love of home, of children, and of domestic duties are the only passion they feel," while yet another writer praised female frigidity as "a virtue to be cultivated, and sexual coldness as a condition to be desired."[77]

In his study of the family in nineteenth-century America, John Demos concludes that the cult of true womanhood was half of the most systematic differentiation of sex roles in the nation's history, the other half being the masculinity cult. Men, too, were typecast to the point of caricature as belonging first and always to the world of affairs and, as Demos notes, "if this was their sphere, it called forth an appropriate character, which included strength, cunning, inventiveness, endurance—a whole range of traits henceforth defined as exclusively 'masculine.'...Among their other attitudes, American men...were saddled with a heavy burden of libido. Sexual desire was regarded as an exclusively male, *and mostly unfortunate*, phenomenon. Women, in their purity, were supposed to be passionless—not merely chaste, but literally devoid of sexual feelings. This complex of ideas was an invention of the age, with massive behavioral consequences."[78] Thus, while sexual desire was attributed to males, the avoidance of heterosexual relationships made that desire not just mostly, but ironically, unfortunate, and men first repressed, then sublimated sexual energy into other, nonsexual areas to achieve, paradoxically, an asexual masculinity. Again, Degler's claim that male ideology was not acted upon by most men seems beside the point. They saw women and themselves in particular ways and, keeping in mind the whole gynecology syndrome and the mytho-symbolic implications of the westward movement, they often acted, too.

Those same women, however, whose development was restricted by fiat not only became "nature's nuns" but superior mothers as well, providing whatever was asked of them and expecting little in return beyond a familial affection. And because of the taboo on heterosexual equality enforced by males, American men unwittingly placed themselves in the dual and contradictory role of patriarch and eternal child, one the breadwinner, the other the grateful recipient of motherly attention. In both roles he was safe from the threats he saw in women: for the stern provider, they were helpless children; for the adult turned child, they were providers of another kind who would attend to his comforts without distracting him with unmotherly demands. In his neurotic dualism, the male gained further reinforcement of his autonomy in the fact that, unconsciously at least, any attempt at a genuine heterosexual relationship would be tantamount to incest.

A noteworthy personification of the adult-child who both rejects women and needs them is the main character in Harold Frederic's novel *The Damnation of Theron Ware*, set in post-bellum America. As a white, Protestant minister and as a husband, Ware is an authority figure in the world he inhabits, yet he is thoroughly boyish, too, and the tension created between these two aspects of his personality provides the psychological center of the novel. In short, he is the neurotic American male who condescends to women as inferior beings (he tacitly agrees with the sinister Ledsmar's claim that females "are not metaphysical people. They do not easily follow abstractions")[79] but he also needs the various women in the novel as mother-figures: his wife, Alice, to care for his domestic wants; Celia Madden, to teach him the wonders of the world and after whom Ware tags like a lovesick boy; and Sister Soulsby, to instruct him in how to be successful and to comfort him when he has been crushed by the reality of his mistakes. Yet a bona fide sexual relationship is impossible with any of these women because in Ware's mind they are either repugnant (Alice), overwhelming (Celia), or a source of practical guidance (Sister Soulsby). Alice in particular represents a limited life, a smothering domesticity, once Ware has discovered worldliness, and he comes to view her not as a woman but as a representative of a type of woman: "Wives, with their limited grasp of the realities of life, were always expecting their husbands to do things which it turned out not to be feasible for them to do. The customary male animal spent a considerable part of his life in explaining to his mate why it had been necessary to disappoint or upset her little plans for his comings and goings. It was in the very nature of things that it should be so" (p. 217).

It is also, however, in the nature of things for Ware, the eternal boy, not only to find substitute mother-figures in other women but to recognize in a priest the image of triumphant masculinity:

> He looked at the priest, and had a quaint sensation of feeling as a romantic woman must feel in the presence of a specially impressive masculine personality. It was indeed strange that this soft-voiced, portly creature in a gown, with his white, fat hands and his feline suavity of manner, should produce such a commanding and unique effect of virility. No doubt this was a part of the great sex mystery which historically surrounded the figure of the celibate priest as with an atmosphere. Women had always been prostrating themselves before it. Theron, watching his companion's full, pallid face in the lamp-light, tried to fancy himself in the priest's place, looking down upon these worshipping female forms. [Pp. 285-86]

The "great sex mystery" to which Ware refers involves Father Forbes's asexual autonomy, his ability to hold power over his female parishioners precisely because he has avoided, so far as Ware can perceive, any heterosexual entanglements. The priest is obligated to no women, only served by them, and a basic distinction Ware makes between his own weakened state and Father Forbes's position of strength is that one man is married while the other is not. Also unsettling for Ware, an established WASP, is the fact that the priest is not just a powerful man but a powerful Irish Catholic, too, one who has obviously lodged himself in the culture and must be accounted for.

The novel ends with the Wares going west so that he might be born again in real estate, and Alice, who has "had it pretty well taken out of me" (p. 346), wonders if her husband will

always be a backslider, to which Sister Soulsby replies that "he'll
be just an average kind of man,—a little sore about some things,
a little wiser than he was about some others"(p. 346). Yet Ware
already envisions a new kind of power awaiting him in the
Washington Territory, that of a senator, and when the Soulsbys
say they will visit the Wares in the nation's capital, Alice can
only respond with "Oh, it isn't likely I would come East. Most
probably I'd be left to amuse myself in Seattle" (p. 349): a recognition of her limited role in her husband's life and her ultimate
rejection should he ever pursue success in the affairs of the
world. He will become, to the extent possible for a married man,
a celibate whose virility, like Father Forbes's, relies on detachment and the "great sex mystery" of the masculine mystique
that Theron Ware found so compelling.

The man-child who neutered his wife by turning her into a
mother-figure tested and proved his masculinity outside the home
among other males, and thus the greatest literary contribution
to the American imagination involves a boy and his male companion—Huckleberry Finn and Tom Sawyer—who flee female
symbols of civilization (the widow Douglas and Miss Watson,
Aunt Polly and Aunt Sally, respectively) but who would never
deliberately offend these women as their surrogate mothers.
Fiedler has observed that "*all* American boys belong to mother,"
and "*to betray the mother*—to deny her like the young rogue in
The Prince and the Pauper—this is the unforgivable sin."[80] In assessing Becky Thatcher as the Good Girl who calls Tom Sawyer
a bad boy out of affection, Fiedler concludes that

> it is the fate of the Good Good Girl (who must suffer, too, like
> the more mature savior-figures before her) to love such boys
> precisely because they play hooky, cuss, steal in a mild sort of a
> way, dream of violence. Where taboos forbid the expression of
> sexuality such delinquency is a declaration of maleness. The Good
> Bad Boy is, of course, America's vision of itself, crude and unruly
> in his beginnings, but endowed by his creator with an instinctive
> sense of what is right. Sexually as pure as any milky maiden, he
> is a roughneck all the same, at once potent and submissive, made
> to be reformed by the right woman.[81]

If Becky Thatcher is a miniature portrait of adult ladies who suffer over the foibles of their men—from Dame Van Winkle on—then Huck and Tom are likewise examples of adult male behavior and reactions to the women whose highest calling is both to dote on and to provide moral discipline to restless men. They are boys even as Twain's characters are boys, and they run away from the female home (Becky, if not a mother, is at least a tongue-clucking sister) only to return to it for relief from the trials and terrors of the male world. Immediately, however, plans are made for the next flight into the wilderness beyond the domestic sphere of influence, and Huck decides to "light out for the Territory ahead of the rest, because Aunt Sally she's going to adopt me and civilize me and I can't stand it."[82] The completion of one flight-and-return cycle to begin another takes several weeks in Twain's and perhaps America's greatest novel, but it represents by way of metaphor a similar, cyclical course followed by American men every working day of the year as they did "naughty" or coarse things according to their maleness, then were chided and cared for by their motherly wives and daughters who were, of course, learning to become motherly wives themselves.

These men found the image of the forgiving mother necessary to keep intact "an imaginary American commonwealth of boy children, camerados at work and play," and as a product of his culture, the American writer in the nineteenth century was dismayed by marriage and passion because "both. . .impugn the image of woman as mother, mean the abandonment of childhood."[83] Thus, Fiedler concludes,

> there is no authentic American who would not rather be Jack than the Giant, which is to say, who would not choose to be "one of the boys" to the very end. The ideal American postulates himself as the fatherless man, the eternal son of the mother. . . . There is finally no heterosexual solution which the American psyche finds completely satisfactory, no imagined or real consummation between man and woman found worthy of standing in our fiction for the healing of the breach between consciousness and unconsciousness, reason and impulse, society and nature. Yet in no nation in the world are those cleavages more deeply felt, declared, indeed, in the very pattern of historical life, visibly represented by the frontier. . . . The quest which has distinguished our fiction

from Brockden Brown and Cooper, through Poe and Melville and Twain, to Faulkner and Hemingway is the search for an innocent substitute for adulterous passion and marriage alike.[84]

That substitute—the frontier, the marketplace, or both—and the search for it provided the Jacksonian democrat and his sons with their *raison d'être*, their ultimate definition of freedom from forces no longer foreign but domestic.

In a culture whose values were determined by and oriented toward men, women by and large accepted their own dual appointment as "nature's nuns" and magnificent mothers since, as one woman wrote, they had

> more of the motherly nature than the conjugal about them.... Their husbands are to them only children of larger growth, to be loved and cared for very much in the same way as their real children. It is the motherly element which is the hope, and is to be the salvation of the world. The higher a woman rises in moral and intellectual culture, the more is the sensual refined away from her nature, and the more pure and perfect and predominating becomes her motherhood. The real woman regards all men, be they older or younger than herself, not as possible lovers, but as a sort of step-sons, towards whom her heart goes out in motherly tenderness.[85]

It is not surprising, therefore, that in the twentieth century George Santayana, himself a product of a nineteenth-century upbringing, would reflect on the American's perpetual state of arrested adolescence:

> The American is wonderfully alive; and his vitality, not having often found a suitable outlet, makes him appear agitated on the surface; he is always letting off an unnecessarily loud blast of steam. Yet his vitality is not superficial; it is inwardly prompted, and as sensitive and quick as a magnetic needle.... He seems to bear lightly the sorrowful burden of human knowledge. In a word, he is young.... Trite and rigid bits of morality and religion, with much seemly and antique political lore, remain axiomatic in him, as in the mind of a child.... A good young man is naturally conservative and loyal on all those subjects which his experience has not brought to a test; advanced opinions on politics, marriage,

or literature are comparatively rare in America; they are left for the ladies to discuss, and usually to condemn, while the men get on with their work. In spite of what is old-fashioned in his more general ideas, the American is unmistakably young.[86]

The dual role men assumed in adulthood—the patriarchal child—was not an aberration of their youth but a natural extension of it. The psychosexual rite of passage for young men in Victorian America was a struggle between conflicting forces, one the compelling sexual urges they could not deny, the other a sense of purity they could not do without, and this dilemma had to be accommodated if they hoped to enter the world of true men. As part of their preparation, male adolescents were indoctrinated against their biological impulses with constant reminders that carnality was a sin as well as an invitation to disease and that "self-abuse" would, according to the leading medical moralists of the time, cause laziness, bad posture, acne, loss of appetite, daydreaming, epilepsy, cardiovascular sluggishness, and insanity. Sylvester Graham, for example, advised young men that "he who in any manner endeavours to excite the sensual appetites, and arouse the unchaste passions of youth, is one of the most heinous offenders against the welfare of mankind," and the sisters Catharine Beecher and Harriet Beecher Stowe coauthored an advice book for women in which they declared that "a wise mother will be especially careful that her sons are trained to modesty and purity of mind. . . . There is no necessity for explanations on this point any further than this: that certain parts of the body are not to be touched except for purposes of cleanliness, and that the most dreadful suffering comes from disobeying these commands. So in regard to practices and sins of which a young child will sometimes inquire, the wise parent will say, that this is what children cannot understand, and about which they must not talk or ask questions."[87]

Yet the ideal of purity was just that, an ideal, and thus young men about to enter adulthood and the world of work were encouraged to seek wives as a realistic compromise between the destructive potential of their sexuality and the impossibility of denying that sexuality altogether. Woman, properly circumscribed, could easily remain virginal, if not a virgin, in marriage since her sexual needs were minimal to begin with, and her influence would appease his sexual needs enough to protect him from his own base impulses:

> Purity, considered as a moral imperative, set up a dilemma which was hard to resolve. Woman must preserve her virtue until marriage and marriage was necessary for her happiness. Yet marriage was, literally, an end to innocence. She was told not to question this dilemma, but simply to accept it. Submission was perhaps the most feminine virtue expected of women. Men were supposed to be religious, although they rarely had time for it, and supposed to be pure, although it came awfully hard to them, but men were the movers, the doers, the actors. Women were the passive, submissive responders.[88]

In adulthood, therefore, as in youth, men were obliged to satisfy two roles polarizing the personality to comply with the prerequisites for manliness—calculated aggressiveness and a purity approximating the sexless child's—and sublimating the bulk of their energies to the world beyond the home where manliness was tested day by day. Referring to this wild-oats-and-purity syndrome, Peter Filene concludes that it "formed a contradictory masculine mythology. Many men were therefore confused, others chose a righteous and anxious pursuit of purity, and still others—having come to terms with their consciences—quietly practiced the double standard. But no position was entirely comfortable, because no man escaped the ambivalent teachings of 'manliness.' "[89] As Filene points out, this sexual dilemma among males was not unique to the nineteenth century since it was as old as America and the Christian injunctions against promiscuity. Yet while the earliest Puritans punished adultery and fined a "surprisingly large number of pregnant brides...they also acknowledged sexual desire within marriage to be a part of God's creation and therefore to be enjoyed along with His other gifts. Nineteenth-century Victorians redefined sexuality into a 'base,' disquieting, almost disgusting emotion; they confined it so rigorously to the realm of the private and unmentionable and mysterious that they suffered it with divinity, but also shame."[90]

Filene traces this Victorian prudery to England where, in reaction to the French Revolution, a movement began within the
middle class to preserve social and political stability by "constraining the lower (and also the upper) classes within safe bounds
of behavior. Evangelical religion added its ascetic weight to the
bourgeois constraint of the lower classes."[91] Within a few decades, this Victorian ethos crossed the Atlantic where middle class
spokesmen—e.g., doctors, ministers, businessmen, social Darwinists—adopted it in an effort to sustain their status over foreigners, native minorities, and women, a few of whom were
beginning to chafe for more power. Thus, Filene concludes,
"according to the Victorian ethic, sexuality should be disciplined
not only by law, but also by shame, and then concealed beneath
silence as heavy as corsets and topcoats."[92] In this way, men
believed their autonomy was inviolate. Sex, a wanton expenditure of energy and power, had to be repressed in males while
in women it had to be denied or ignored so that they might
become the fleshless guardian angels of the male world, a world
feeling guilt and shame over actual sexuality but pride in the
things achieved via sublimated sexual energy in the West and
on Wall Street.

In "nature's nuns," the infantile or adolescent male, and the
endless sentimental tributes paid to motherhood lies evidence
supporting Leslie Fiedler's thesis that a distinguishing characteristic of American culture has been the inability to deal with
mature genital love.[93] To have done so would have reduced the
American democrat to a level of equality with the opposite sex
he could not abide and forced him to spend the sexual time and
energy, the virility, he needed to do his own and society's work
in alliance with other males. Profound heterosexual involvement
and progress were mutually contradictory, and the WASP male
had only to cite the sexual conduct of the "inferior races" to
prove his own superior position on the evolutionary scale. Such
matters as their innate intellectual inferiority aside, blacks, Indians, and most immigrants would remain slackers, political and
economic ne'er-do-wells, and, therefore, society's weaklings because they failed to see the value of sexual restraint. In short,
they wasted their vital energies. For a nation on the move and
men in a race with each other, sex was a debilitating force, and

as a turn-of-the-century writer put it, "as long as mankind marries in order to indulge in a licensed sexual intercourse, it will seek happiness in vain. No purely animal pleasure can satisfy its nature, which is striving Godward."[94]

3

THE JACKSONIAN LEGACY

Although the Age of Jackson generally set the course the country would follow for the rest of the century, the moods and the methods Americans adopted along the way were not always the same as those which dominated the 1820s and 1830s. The culture, it would seem, could only expand so far in its boundless optimism before it had to pull back and restore spent energy, if only as a prelude to a renewed sense of boundlessness. This pendulum effect—expansiveness to retrenchment—became apparent by the late 1840s and signalled a major shift in American attitudes, suggesting that while the pendulum continued to move, it was driven by a different force. That is, after mid-century the dominant stroke was that of retrenchment, of consolidation and control, so that what may have appeared on the surface to be another outward-bound phase was not that at all, at least not to the degree it had been in Jackson's time.

The weaker stroke, or change in cultural direction, can be explained by the fact that, unlike Jacksonians who were driven by rampant optimism, Americans from the 1850s on felt an essential cynicism that underscored much of what they did and periodically forced them back into the mold, into the need for order and for authority to check mounting threats of cultural chaos. Thus, the years immediately preceding the Civil War were characterized by a bona fide reaction against egalitarian ideals at home as well as disillusionment over political events abroad. By contrast, the late 1860s and the early 1870s seemed to be another period of limitless possibilities—of industrialization, of railroads spanning the continent by 1869, of waves of migrants moving west. Yet beneath all this growth lay the desire to circumscribe the land with tracks and boundaries, to tame unruliness with civilization's constraints, and skillfully to exploit both the marketplace and natural resources for great gains in return. This underlying mood of containment and conquest, masked for a time by geographical and economic diffusion, congealed in the 1880s when urban living conditions, labor strife, various reform movements, and massive immigration stimulated among WASPs in power a reactionary mentality geared to the preservation of the species. Thus, the pendulum had swung once again, but it did not signify a major cultural shift so much as it revealed, once again, a pervasive mood in American life since the end of the Age of Jackson.

CULTURAL RETRENCHMENT AND
AN AGE OF CYNICISM

By the middle of the nineteenth century, much of the enthusiasm of the Age of Jackson had played itself out, and Americans began seeking ways to stabilize themselves and the culture to deal with the rapid change in social, economic, and political institutions together with the unprecedented mobility and culture shock that had characterized American life after 1815. Furthermore, they came to realize that unrestrained democracy and rampant nationalism would solve neither their own problems nor the world's, and cultural ferment must, therefore, at some point be checked so that progress could be pursued in a more orderly fashion. The end of the Mexican War in 1848 and the failure of various revolutions in Europe during the same decade suggested to Americans that this nation had reached its natural limits geographically and that democracy was not always the inevitable outcome of upheaval. Indeed, democracy might disappear altogether in endless turmoil, a lesson Americans took to heart as their jubilation over events abroad—e.g., the Hungarian Revolution and the downfall of King Louis Philippe in 1848—dwindled in the face of continued despotism in Europe. Thus, according to John Higham, outside the proslavery states "it was commonly assumed by the late 1850's that the Union was complete," and Americans began to regard revolution and unassimilable change as not the best means to gain democratic ends, but as anarchistic attempts to undermine the republic.[1]

The urge to unify, to set limits on raucous individualism and to extract order out of chaos, helps to explain northern animosity toward southern demands for autonomy before and during the Civil War as well as some of the results of that great struggle: emancipated blacks neither equal nor free; an ineffective effort at genuine reconstruction; a general erosion of democratic, egalitarian values; and a newfound respect for institutional authority and discipline.[2] Thus, a cultural mood in the 1850s leading up to the war was intensified by the conflict, and in the post-bellum decades, America experienced an age of cynicism toward earlier democratic ideals as those in power manipulated others with impunity and those without power gritted their way through recessions, riots, and strikes. Men pooled their efforts—managerial cartels and labor movements alike—to obtain what personal initiative alone could not procure. As Robert Wiebe has pointed out, by the 1880s "the very process of urban living generated its own special values. The individualism and casual cooperation of the towns still had their place in a city. But new virtues—regularity, systems, continuity—clashed increasingly with the old. The city dweller could never protect his home from fire or rid his street of garbage by the spontaneous voluntarism that had raised cabins along the frontier."[3] That is, men felt that organization, direction, and collective security were better suited to gaining self-fulfillment and security in a massive, complex society even though tribute was still paid to the mythical, rugged individual.

Rapidly becoming industrialized and overcrowded, the cities were centers of concern for stability, control, and more clearly defined social strata. The combination of squalor, black migration northward, and a continuing influx of foreigners threatened to dilute traditional WASP power in a melting pot reputed to contain nothing better than illiteracy, paganism or papism, and wasteful sexual habits producing disease, slothfulness, and a burdensome population:

> The presumed passing of the frontier subtly wove a thread of uneasiness through many...late-nineteenth-century themes. ...Early in the eighties the conquest of the Plains had served as evidence of America's virility, the fulfillment of one destiny promising grander ones to come. It was the perspective of the threatened community that turned victory into the preface for defeat. When anxious Americans paired the congested cities with dwindling opportunities along the frontier, urban centers seemed that much more turgid, and the prospects of an explosion that much more ominous. Advocates of immigration restriction cited the scarcity of free land as one more reason why the nation could no longer leave its doors open.[4]

The threat of dark-skinned people—first perceived on a widespread basis before the Civil War—was now intolerable, and WASPs reacted accordingly.

Concerning sexuality in particular, the shift in cultural mood from expansiveness and infinite possibilities to retrenchment and constraint was manifested in a parallel attitude toward the expenditure of energy. Thus, in the Gilded Age the call for modified individualism and the careful management of complicated social and economic systems had its psychosexual corollary in attitudes that have defined the age as Victorian. Energy, sexual and otherwise, was too valuable to be spent carelessly, and the men who would succeed were no longer unrestrained individualists but those capable of thrift (or, in psychological terminology, repression) and a dispassionate, machine-like efficiency: a reincarnation into broader, cultural terms of childhood adjurations against the wasteful, debilitating effects of masturbation from men such as Sylvester Graham. And in an age when power was measured by wealth, wealth was obtained through management, and all three relied on intricate alliances between men, the self-reliant, expansive man of a former age—like the democratic idealist or agitator—was outmoded or even a dangerous threat to the orderly, well-managed progress of society. This attitude would periodically rise and fall during the decades after mid-century, but it was always there, either on the surface (e.g., the 1850s and 1880s) or just beneath it (e.g., the 1860s and 1870s).

Post-bellum America was in general the age of the entrepreneur and the political boss, when profit and power signalled a peculiar asexual prowess because time and sublimated sexuality were turned to these ends and applied with the skill and care of the specialist. Thorstein Veblen, for example, noted a marked difference between tycoons in the first half of the nineteenth century and those who moved into the Civil War with empires in mind. As he explains it, entrepreneurs in the age of Jackson— first-generation magnates—were free-wheeling types whose sweeping, often ludicrous, business adventures carried them far afield of standard financial practices. They were wildcat speculators, boom-or-bust investors who, after mid-century, "fell to second rank...as being irresponsible, fanciful project-makers, footloose adventurers....Such men are persons whom it is not for the safe and sane Captains of the newer type to countenance."[5] Veblen's explanation for the rise of a new kind of captain of industry, though given in strictly business terms, has implications for the culture at large, and he maintains that "by about the middle of the nineteenth century...industries were beginning to be inordinately productive, as rated in terms of what the traffic would bear....Free-swung production, approaching the full productive capacity of the equipment and available man-power, was no longer to be tolerated in ordinary times. It became ever more imperative to observe a duly graduated moderation."[6] In other words, as America began to develop as an industrial society, success was to be had by the man capable of careful planning and calculated acquisition, the man who could control his resources and energy rather than waste them. An editorial in the *Nation* in 1870 declared that "a man is morally ruined, in the eyes of the economist, when he runs about whoremongering, instead of working at his calling and supporting his wife and children; he is morally ruined, in the eyes of the theologian, when he disobeys God's law. But there is nothing necessarily incompatible in the two views."[7] Various secular specialists were experts in morality, too, and Nathan G. Hale has explained that

> some physicians taught a sexual hygiene that explicitly united economic and religious motives. The most devout developed the strictest standards of sexual discipline. . . . Doctors, articulating the ideals of the industrious middle and upper classes, subordinated sexual gratification to family affection and social achievement. Physicians developed models for the manly man and the womanly woman that prescribed optimally healthy sexual behavior. The central doctrine of this "civilized" sexual discipline held that energy must be carefully husbanded and that weakening excesses be avoided. Physicians often likened bodily energy to a stock of goods, or more commonly, to a bank account. Its fixed and limited quantity easily could be exhausted unless judiciously replenished. All otiose gratification therefore was undesirable, and sexual continence, or self-restraint, was a logical necessity.[8]

Leading businessmen, therefore, advocated sperm retention as a means of achieving manliness and wealth, a concept set forth by Dr. J. H. Kellogg, the cereal king, in his *Plain Facts for Both Sexes*, first published in 1879. Among other things, Kellogg reported the amazing "vigor and vitality" of an eighty-year-old man who had been injected with fluids from the sex glands of a male rabbit.[9]

In their study of industrial America, Thomas C. Cochran and William Miller corroborate Veblen's earlier assessment from a slightly different angle, which places the business mind in a social context:

> Tireless, efficient, often requiring but the cheapest unskilled labor to tend it, the machine was the creator of industrial wealth. In a country expanding as rapidly as the United States in mid-century, its use could be extended almost without limit to supply the needs of a rich and voracious market. Yet under a system of free competition. . . there were dangers in mechanization so great that periodically the capital of producers was consumed, turning lively enterprises into failures almost overnight, turning competition into cutthroat channels, and encouraging the growth of monopolies.[10]

Complex economic systems, like the machines that served them, had to be tended to by men who understood them to avoid or to repair major breakdowns, and by the late 1870s the managers of the nation's wealth looked with skepticism on their immediate predecessors who, though managers themselves and motivated by the need to control and to acquire, had employed methods reminiscent of an unrestrained, Jacksonian America. They had, in Cochran and Miller's words, "remorselessly... exploited precious resources, stripping incomparable forests, leaving gaping holes in mountain sides to mark exhausted mines, dotting with abandoned derricks oil fields drained of petroleum and natural gas. In reckless haste, they constructed railroads through the wilderness, and immense factories to supply the needs of millions yet unborn."[11] This enormous expenditure of energy—however motivated—could not go on indefinitely, and in the latter decades of the century "a new order began to emerge out of the chaos of brutal competition. Entrepreneurs were learning the profitable lessons of specialized and standardized production, of geographical concentration of plants, of centralized management. Corporations at war were learning that combination was a surer way to wealth and power."[12]

This movement toward concentration and combination, toward a belief that bigness was best, was not just a phenomenon of the business world but an indication of a widespread cultural attitude. And because the culture no longer placed its faith in the limitless potential of the individual democrat moving out from the centers of power but in accumulated power and the fitness of those men in charge, WASP males often projected their anxieties in the opposite direction, too. That is, once the full implications of the doctrine of laissez-faire and the Jacksonian principle of unfettered competition had been revealed and used as rationalizations for concentrated power, men did not fear authority but aspired to it. Now threats came from the outside, from those who would reduce power rather than wield it—well-bred gentlemen whose social status no longer carried with it automatic influence, reformers, do-gooders, and moralistic idealists—and the *nouveau riche* of the Gilded Age imitated their fathers insofar as they rejected these threats as effeminate and degenerate. In brief, the cultural shift from expansiveness to retrenchment after 1850—with what appeared to be a brief lapse into boundlessness between 1865 and the mid-1870s—did not eliminate or even significantly reduce the WASP male's overweening sense of masculinity but caused him instead to reassert the manliness ethos in keeping with the times and to project his psychosexual anxieties in different directions. A theme in American life that was basically Jacksonian in its origins was thus repeated in the latter decades of the nineteenth century with variations—and cynical overtones—conducive to the changing cultural mood.

THE NEO-JACKSONIAN RESPONSE

The Protestant ethic concerning work and virtue—still more or less intact during Jackson's time—was translated during and after the Civil War to mean that work, however unvirtuous it might appear, produced virtue nonetheless in the form of power, money, and status. These in turn were comments on the men who held them and made them the manliest of all, a concept suggesting a sublimated sexuality with economic, political, and social potency the measures of virtue or, more accurately perhaps, virility. Stanley Diamond has shown that wealth and power are civilized counterbalances for fear of impotence:

> The dynamics of archaic civilization reveal the pathology of wealth—wealth as power, or luxury as "well being"—and the inadequacy of the distribution of wealth. By 3000 B.C. in the Middle East, such rationalizations for the state, which also apply to monopoly capitalism, are apparent. As Marx understood, the processes of state formation and function are generalizable beyond the specific form of the state. The critical question, then, is that of the socio-economic exploitation and the concomitant loss of the cultural creativity and autonomy of the vast majority of human beings. Conspicuous extortion from worker and peasant was a confirmation of power; but power, so reified, not only confirmed social status, it also displaced anxiety about the actual powerlessness of the privileged, which was a result of the loss of their direct command of the environment. The sheer accumulation of wealth, the antithesis of primitive customary usage, was thus compensatory, a sign of the fear of impotence. It is a

response of the alienated in pursuit of security; the manipulation
of people is substituted for the command of things. As civilization
spreads and deepens, it is ultimately man's self, his species, which
is imperialized. [13]

In pursuit of cultural as well as financial security, the kings
of commerce—Rockefeller, Carnegie, Vanderbilt, Morgan, Gould,
et al.—were archetypal figures, and the culture that tolerated,
if not accepted, their excesses did so because such men represented in thought and deed what Richard Hofstadter has called
"an age of cynicism,"[14] an age whose memory reached back to
Jeffersonian and Jacksonian idealism but whose experience included the cultural chaos of ante-bellum America: a divisive war,
an assassinated president, reconstruction, urban blight, the realities of living by the factory system, and massive immigration.
The men who owned the factories and ran the cities "made a
mockery of the ideals of the simple gentry who imagined that
the nation's development could take place with dignity and restraint under the regime of laissez-faire. Their exploits created
the moral atmosphere that caused such an honorable conservative of the old school as E. L. Godkin to say: 'I came here fifty
years ago with high and fine ideals about America.... They are
now all shattered, and I have apparently to look elsewhere to
keep even moderate hopes about the human race alive.' "[15]

This cynicism, or anxiety, over the uselessness of old ideals
in a modern setting caused men to view practical mindedness
as a manly trait to justify its pursuit, even as it allowed them to
reject idealists and reformers as less than manly specimens in a
new age. As in the Age of Jackson, the process of asserting
masculinity in the Gilded Age involved an unconscious trans-
lating of a cultural situation into psychosexual terms to define
it and then a displacing or projecting of the anxieties of that
situation onto others. Tension was thereby resolved indirectly,
and men felt free to go about their business with the assurance
that they were following their best and natural impulses. Thus,
the cynicism of business and political bosses toward idealism in
the last half of the century made reform not only a difficult task
but a degrading one as well: "Party warhorses, who tended to
identify rapacity with manliness, looked upon 'good' men in

politics as dudes, freaks, immune to the spirit of their time not out of viritue but perversity—'man milliners,' as [Roscoe] Conkling said.... [James G.] Blaine referred to them in a letter to Garfield as 'upstarts, conceited, foolish, vain...noisy but not numerous, pharisaical but not practical, ambitious but not wise, pretentious but not powerful.' "[16] Between the time of Andrew Jackson and the age of the entrepreneur, a curious shift had occurred in the male mind regarding the cultural criteria for manliness, a shift in which the ends were altered though the means remained much the same. Adams's defeat in 1828 can be attributed in part to the belief that he represented intellect, culture, wealth, and status—in short, established authority—and that Old Hickory was the man capable of challenging aristocratic prerogatives or even abolishing authoritarian institutions such as the Bank on behalf of the individual and to meet new conditions. But conditions change, and after the Civil War the children of the Jacksonian era had come of age and now, as men called upon to pull the nation together, they wanted no part of reform. Instead, they wanted power, institutionalized and laden with prerogatives, to accomplish their tasks. Their adversaries, however, like those of Jacksonian democrats, were still conceived of as effeminate and weak-willed because they wished to hamper men from doing what men knew they must do. The shift, then, was from reform as evidence of manliness to hostility toward reform as evidence of manliness.

The question was no longer one of granting the common man the power to make choices and to govern his own destiny, but of retaining that power once it had been amassed by the fittest in the struggle to survive. But in both periods—Jacksonian America and the Gilded Age—the enemy was the same: educated, cultivated men who professed high ideals regardless of the social, political, and economic realities around them. Living outside politics and above the necessity of hard labor, they were quick to point out their own purity and to push for what they felt should be society's, an arrogant and naive position their toughminded adversaries—spokesmen for the cynicism and fear of elitism felt by Americans—were just as quick to attack:

The politicians and bosses found their answer in crying down the superior education and culture of their critics as political liabilities, and in questioning their adequacy for the difficult and dirty work of day-to-day politics. As the politicians put it, they, the bosses and party workers, had to function in the bitter world of reality in which the common people also had to live and earn their living. This was not the sphere of morals and ideals, of education and culture: it was the hard, masculine sphere of business and politics. The reformers, they said, claimed to be unselfish; but if this was true at all, it was true only because they were alien commentators upon an area of life in which they did not have to work and for which in fact they were unfit. In the hard-driving, competitive, ruthless, materialistic world of the Gilded Age, to be unselfish suggested not purity but a lack of self, a lack of capacity for grappling with reality, a lack of assertion, of masculinity. Invoking a well-established preconception of the American male, the politicians argued that culture is impractical and men of culture are ineffectual, that culture is feminine and cultivated men tend to be effeminate.[17]

Yet Hofstadter's assessment of anti-intellectualism in the Gilded Age, cogent and informative as it is in recognizing a pervasive sense of masculinity at work, does not pursue the psychological implications of the manliness ethos and without them, events are sometimes discussed without at least a potential explanation for causes. That is, women were the obvious, sometimes threatening, opposite of men, and males would, therefore, often displace their fear of being womanized or symbolically emasculated not by direct attacks against women but by describing male opponents in female terms. This projection mechanism not only demeaned its male victims in the eyes of other men but also vented a largely unconscious male distrust of women. And in both instances, the manliness of the initiator and his allies was confirmed and with it, their positions on the issues they addressed in this manner.

The assault on intellect and culture thus went far beyond the question of practicality in dealing with grim realities and centered on the wispy character of the reformers themselves, men of manners and "namby-pamby, goody-goody gentlemen" who "sip cold tea" and were, therefore, unmasculine.[18] Senator J. J. Ingalls of Kansas referred to reformers as "the third sex" and declared that "they have two recognized functions. They sing falsetto, and they are usually selected as the guardians of the seraglios of Oriental despots."[19] Elsewhere, Ingalls described idealistic reformers as "effeminate without being either masculine or feminine; unable to beget or to bear; possessing neither fecundity nor virility; endowed with the contempt of men and the derision of women, and doomed to sterility, isolation, and extinction."[20] Reformers and cultivated men were, according to influential adherents of the manliness ethos, impotent sissies at best, sexual mutations at worst.

Such psychosexual assaults reveal as much about the attackers as they were intended to reveal about those under attack and reinforce the concept of the sublimation of male sexuality into power, politics, and rampant materialism. In other words, the egalitarian paradox of Jacksonianism—equality versus anonymity—had, by the latter half of the century, been played out to what the strongest believed was a satisfactory conclusion: equality was an idealistic and therefore foolish contradiction of a basic law of nature while anonymity (Ingalls's "sterility, isolation, and extinction") indicated masculine weakness at the deepest psychological levels. The paradox, like the idealism that had fostered it, was swept aside, and such seemingly simple reform ideas as honesty in business and politics posed a psychosexual threat to the bosses every bit as intimidating as the assaults they waged against the reformers.

To yield to outmoded notions of ethics and virtue would be to sacrifice not only power, money, and possessions but the masculinity they helped to define. And as leaders for an age, the robber barons and slick politicians were in many ways representative of American cynicism in general. That is, no matter how vicious their condemnations of do-gooders might have been, such charges were, in a certain sense, accurate. While the reformers were concerned with such nebulous issues as public morality, the farmer was concerned with making ends meet, with holding onto his land in the face of deflated prices for his goods, rising prices for his equipment, and monopolies which caused both. In addition, massive industrialism after the Civil War brought all the attendant evils confronting every rapidly industrialized society: low wages, long hours, slums, and labor struggles usually won by management with ugly, brutal moves. As Wiebe points out, management—preoccupied with forging empires—tried to ignore cultural discord in the immediate post-war years but then reacted decisively against dissension as it took form in the Knights of Labor and expressed itself in the notorious Haymarket Riot:

> Because many of the men in power tried initially to ignore signs of upheaval . . . they moved through it that much more swiftly and savagely. Moreover, their themes of distress, while also phrased in the language of individualism and unity, had a distinctive ring. In the baldest sense, they came to fear that in a democratic society the people might rule. Individualism, except as a mode of implicit comtempt for the scattered sheep below, almost always referred to the rights of an elite to retain what they held and to acquire more; cohesion meant an imposed order, one that would necessitate a sharp-edged enforcement. Rather than anticipating the good that would eventually arise from crisis, they wanted to quash all disorder now, to forestall catastrophe by fitting society into a safe, sturdy mold. . . . An urban leadership, already uneasy over the strange population swelling about them, reacted to the "great uprising of labor" in the mid-eighties as if an army of swords had been unsheathed. With incredible exaggeration, they interpreted the Knights of Labor as disciplined mass sedition and the brief epidemic of local labor parties in 1886 and 1887 as a preface to political revolution.[21]

Several depressions during the last three decades of the century further confirmed the common man in his bitterness, and to believe that public morality—whatever it meant—could solve his problems was not only absurd, it was insulting. As Hofstadter has written, "in politics the reformers were both isolated and sterile. Intellectuals, obsessed with the abstract ideal of public service, businessmen tired of the cost of graft, patricians worried about the need of honesty in government, they did not know the people, and the people, with good reason, did not know them."[22] Thus, the cynicism of the industrialists represented the massive cynicism of the time. To the manager, reform was both a personal and a professional threat; to the farmer and wage earner, reform was just idle nonsense.

Well-organized reform movements were, therefore, few and futile during the age of the spoilsmen, and such liberal gestures within the Republican party as the nomination of Horace Greeley for president in 1872 and the Mugwump defection in 1884 were little more than tokenisms. Greeley fell before a corrupted Grant in the worst defeat of a presidential candidate in the history of the office, and the Mugwump's support of Cleveland rather than Blaine only reaffirmed conservatism over undeniable corruption. Likewise, reform legislation such as the Interstate Commerce Act and the Sherman Anti-Trust Act had no teeth at the time for the simple reason that many of the legislators who passed them and the officials who were supposed to enforce them were committed to big business and the men who made business big. One of the ironies of the age lay in the fact that even when reform was attempted, the ineffectual results could only strengthen the magnates' belief that they were the fittest among all men and that reformers were effeminate and impotent by comparison.

The derisive counterattacks on moralists and idealists hit full stride in the years following the Republican reform movement in 1872. During the New York State Republican convention of 1877, Roscoe Conkling debunked the reformer George William Curtis, educated in Europe, editor of *Harper's*, and a close friend of many New England intellectuals and artists: "Who are these men who, in newspapers and elsewhere, are cracking their whips over Republicans and playing school-master to the Republican party and its conscience and convictions? Some of them are the man-milliners, the dilettanti and carpet knights of politics....They forget that parties are not built by deportment, or by ladies' magazines, or by gush."[23] Conkling's abuse of Curtis stuck, especially the term "man-milliners," and others took up where Conkling left off. One newspaper reported an account of "a smart boy named Curtis, who parted his hair in the middle like a girl," lived among women only, and was beaten up by the manly Conkling, to the horror of Curtis's female relatives and friends.[24] Curtis, and men like him, were mocked for hiding behind women's skirts or, in psychological terms, for not rejecting the female super-ego when dealing in the affairs of men. Regarding this point, it is worth noting that in 1876—the year

before Conkling's condemnation of Curtis and a period of great
anti-idealism in general—the Statue of Liberty became an American cultural icon embodying the female virtues of compassion
and humanitarian concern. In a gesture only too fitting, she was
brought to this country from Europe—the rejected father—as a
symbolic reminder of what the American Revolution had accomplished, and she has lodged herself in the national imagination
as the personification of motherly affection that American men
consciously, and conscientiously, worship as well as the female
super-ego that they unconsciously resist.

The flamboyant charges laid against reformers by Ingalls and
Conkling contained the attitudes of their peers, of course, but
they also expressed the popular belief that political life was for
males and that women must be excluded for their own good
since success in politics (as in business) was a test of masculinity.
Anything that smacked of its opposite signalled both professional and personal—i.e., sexual—failure. Such generosity toward women, supposedly intended to shelter them from the
sleaziness of the male world, was in fact a profound fear of
women who, given the vote or any other chance, would displace
men in their own territory. Women "would become masculine,
just as men became feminine when they espoused reform. Horace Bushnell suggested that if women got the vote and kept it
for hundreds of years, 'the very look and temperament of women
will be altered.' The appearance of women would be sharp, their
bodies wiry, their voices shrill, their actions angular and abrupt,
and full of self-assertion, will, boldness, and eagerness for place
and power."[25] In *Heiress of All the Ages*, William Wasserstrom
states that "ordinarily, the [genteel] tradition is noted for its
adherence to the twin principles of manliness and womanliness.
Rooted in the eighteenth-century idea about natural nobility,
manliness signified a state of the soul which negated the claims
of the body; womanliness resulted when the body was eliminated."[26] In other words, so long as women remained soft, pli-
able, and without opinions on manly matters, they could pursue
morality, culture, and rarefied ideas as mothers and wives. Likewise, men who wished to make their mark in the world could
not be distracted by women and sex, an attitude encompassed
by Peter Filene's contention that Victorian prudery had its origins

in England as a frenzied response to the French Revolution. Efforts by Englishmen to restrain the upper and lower classes within acceptable limits of behavior were taken up in America a few decades later, and by the late nineteenth century the Victorian code prescribed that sexuality should be suppressed by law, laden with shame, and smothered "beneath silence as heavy as corsets and topcoats."[27]

Veblen's investigation of cultural attitudes in nineteenth-century America includes some reflections on dress and manners as manifestations of conspicuous consumption and conspicuous leisure, "occupations" undertaken by middle and upper class women as avatars of their husbands' economic prowess. Corseted and concealed by layers of elaborate clothing, women were confined both literally and symbolically, their "proper sphere" an inevitable result of the tacit bargain first struck between the sexes during the Age of Jackson. That bargain, a cultural *quid pro quo*, was elaborately expressed during the Gilded Age and underscores the fact that the manliness ethos not only involved the projection of male animus onto man milliners and dilettantes but included the direct relationships between the sexes as well:

> It has come about that obviously productive labor is in a peculiar degree derogatory to respectable women, and therefore special pains should be taken in the construction of women's dress, to impress upon the beholder the fact (often indeed a fiction) that the wearer does not and can not habitually engage in useful work. Propriety requires respectable women to abstain more consistently from useful effort and to make more of a show of leisure than the men of the same social classes. It grates painfully on our nerves to comtemplate the necessity of any well-bred woman's earning a livelihood by useful work. It is not "woman's sphere." Her sphere is within the household, which she should "beautify," and of which she should be the "chief ornament.". . .In the ideal scheme, as it tends to realize itself in the life of the higher pecuniary classes, this attention to conspicuous waste of substance and effort should normally be the sole economic function of the woman.[28]

Sexless women, whose physical activities were often no more strenuous than the ritual of making afternoon calls, fell prey to various forms of invalidism, depression, and "neurasthenia," or hysteria. As a result, they fled in increasing numbers—peaking in the 1880s and 1890s—to all-female health spas, which served a dual function as rehabilitation centers for women and as cultural corollaries to the exclusively male activities of the time.

Relegated to her mythological role as a nonsexual goddess of delicate domesticity, nineteenth-century woman was in effect a possession displayed by the male cult of materialism as evidence of social and economic virility. Far from being a phenomenon unique to America, however, this use of women began, as Veblen points out, in primitive cultures when women were taken from enemies as trophies, a practice that led to the establishment of a type of ownership-marriage, with the male as head of the household.[29] Eventually, ownership-marriage was extended to women other than those stolen from enemies, and "the outcome of emulation under the circumstances of a predatory life, therefore, has been on the one hand a form of marriage resting on coercion, and on the other hand the custom of ownership....Both arise from the desire of the successful men to put their prowess in evidence by exhibiting some durable result of their exploits. Both also minister to that propensity for mastery which pervades all predatory communities."[30]

Veblen's insights into the primitive, predatory nature of male activities illuminates a basic tenet of masculine ideology that declared that just as women unsexed themselves by entering business and politics, so male reformers unsexed themselves by introducing female standards of morality into these fields. The old byword for reformers—"long-haired men and short-haired women"—aptly expressed this popular belief.[31] One of the main themes of Henry James's *The Bostonians* is the fear that the natural masculinity of those who ran the world's affairs would be rendered impotent by meddling, aggressive women. The novel's hero, Basil Ransom, expresses his threatened masculinity in blunt terms as he projects his anxiety onto women and provides in the process an explicit literary example of the castration complex:

> The whole generation is womanized; the masculine tone is passing out of the world; it's a feminine, a nervous, hysterical, chat-

tering, canting age, an age of hollow phrases and false delicacy and exaggerated solicitudes and coddled sensibilities, which, if we don't soon look out, will usher in the region of mediocrity, of the feeblest and flattest and the most pretentious that has ever been. The masculine character, the ability to dare and endure, to know and yet not fear reality, to look the world in the face and take it for what it is—a very queer and partly very base mixture— that is what I want to preserve, or rather, as I may say, recover; and I must tell you that I don't in the least care what becomes of you ladies while I make the attempt![32]

Shortly thereafter, Verena Tarrant asks Ransom, "I am to understand, then, as your last word that you regard us as quite inferior?" to which he replies, "For public, civic uses, absolutely—perfectly weak and second-rate"(p. 348). Oddly enough, however, Ransom's bullying outbursts, though freighted with popular concepts of manliness, could not make *The Bostonians* a book for its time. Wasserstrom explains this curious fact in cultural terms:

James's novel displeased his audience because it separated passion from idealism: the stately middle classes continued to prefer reserve to candor and to admire fiction that shaded its truths with cant. . . . For society, willing to respond to a kind of euphemized virility, was not yet able to admire men who exercised this quality in the matter of love itself. Like James, it respected men of passion; unlike James, it expected these men to adore money and to order their lives according to the gospel of wealth. . . . A generation earlier, men who were self-willed, passionate, who rejected the common morality, had only one recourse. They could head West. After the [Civil] War, however, society gave the highest prestige to those rugged individualists who cornered the markets or created great corporations or, in the fashion of W. L. Newberry of Chicago, consumed large blocks of cheap real estate that were soon to have enormous value.[33]

From the Age of Jackson through the Gilded Age, the American male felt beleaguered by forces that would reduce, or even eliminate, his masculine independence: e.g., unassimilable change, culture shock, and institutional authority in one age; challenges to a masculine authority that had become consolidated, massively acquisitive, and institutionalized in the other. Thus, in the Gilded Age he retained such Jacksonian responses as action over ideas and courage over refinement, yet he reversed another response by claiming the supremacy of nature's law of survival over legal declarations of equality, a reversal necessitated by a cultural change of direction from uncontrolled expansiveness to retrenchment, from unbounded optimism to cynicism. In the last decades of the century, it was time to forsake sentimental tributes to equality, to apply time and energy systematically in the gaining of wealth and prestige. All men may be equal in one sense, but some are more fit than others and that, finally, was the masculine distinction to be made because it was easy to be equal, but tough to survive, and the rewards were there for those who did. Others who wished to alter the process—women or effeminate men—had to be dealt with accordingly, and in its efforts to protect itself by exposing the sexually inferior character of its adversaries, the masculinity cult revealed its own psychosexual frame of mind with a reactionary, anxiety-ridden style.

MASCULINE ALLIANCES AND THE SURVIVAL OF MACHINE-LIKE MEN

In many ways, the Age of Jackson and the Gilded Age were similar because, simply put, one produced the other, and the difference was one of degree, of something that, once born, needed time and a war to mature. And just as the ideas and emotions of one age were suited to the rise of Jackson as symbolic hero, the intellectual, social, and economic inclinations of the other provided the perfect climate of opinion for the industrial barons to grow and to prosper, to embody the wish fulfillment of a nation. In particular, the publication of Darwin's *The Origin of Species* and the work of Herbert Spencer in social philosophy justified what Americans were doing to themselves and to their land, and they accepted the stamp of approval placed by pseudo-Darwinians and Spencerians on something Americans had been experiencing for decades: life was a fierce struggle in which only the fittest survive, and the laws of nature were applicable to the affairs of men. Hofstadter describes the most conspicuous of these men and how they conducted their affairs:

> For the most part they were parvenus, and they behaved with becoming vulgarity; but they were also men of heroic audacity and magnificent exploitative talents—shrewd, energetic, aggressive, rapacious, domineering, insatiable. They directed the proliferation of the country's wealth, they seized its opportunities, they managed its corruption, and from them the era took its tone and color.[34]

By generalizing as he does, Hofstadter apparently avoids some important distinctions, yet his language suggests both the character of society's leaders in the Gilded Age and their motives amid cultural conditions far different from those of Jacksonian America. These men were "shrewd, energetic, aggressive, rapacious, domineering, insatiable"—masculine traits displayed most obviously in the years just after the war—but rather than applying these qualities to more reckless, outward-bound adventures reminiscent of another age and threatening of self and society, they joined forces and "directed," "seized," and "managed" for personal and collective security. While this impulse toward order and control through coalition began, in some instances, as early as the 1860s—e.g., in the building of the transcontinental railroad—it was not revealed as a significant cultural trend until the late 1870s and thereafter. That the impulse existed earlier, however, there can be little doubt.

In other words, post-bellum America "took its tone and color" from the fully developed, masculine prototype whose characteristics had first been sanctioned on a wide scale during the Jacksonian era and whose methods were required in an age of industrialization and, therefore, increasingly complicated social and economic systems not to be handled by the footloose and fancy-free democrat. And while Old Hickory had filled the popular imagination and the White House with a rough-hewn dignity, weaker presidents followed him, including the pathetic Grant who, after the Civil War, could not inspire the nation as an earlier military hero had. Thus, newer and stronger cultural heroes—models for the masses—took over: Huntington, Rockefeller, Vanderbilt, Fisk, Gould, Carnegie, among others of a lesser, more localized stature. Veblen, both an economist and a cultural critic, saw the wealthy as paradigms for the modern democrat:

> The leisure class stands at the head of the social structure in point of reputability; and its manner of life and its standards of worth therefore afford the norm of reputability for the community. The observance of these standards, in some degree of approximation, becomes incumbent upon all classes lower in the scale. In modern civilized communities the lines of demarcation between social classes have grown vague and transient, and wherever this happens the norm of reputability imposed by the upper class extends to the lowest strata. The result is that the members of each stratum accept as their ideal of decency the scheme of life in vogue in the next higher stratum, and bend their energies to live up to that ideal.[35]

Wiebe confirms Veblen's analysis in his discussion of community life and standards in the mid-1870s. Appearances were not always the best gauge of reality, and what may have seemed at first glance to be a great democracy of limitless opportunity was, in fact, a subtle inculcation of upper class values that colored the daily life and the attitudes of American townspeople:

> From a distance the towns exemplified a levelled democracy, sustaining neither an aristocracy of name nor an aristocracy of occupation. Almost anyone with incentive, it seemed, could acquire the skills of a profession....But beneath the flat surface, each community was divided by innumerable, fine gradations. Distinctions that would have eluded an outsider—the precise location of a house, the amount of hired help, the quality of a buggy or a dress—held great import in an otherwise undifferentiated society. In fact, what Thorstein Veblen made famous as "conspicuous consumption" carried a far more exact meaning in the town where everyone looked on and cared than in the cities where only squandered millions would attract attention.[36]

When, therefore, men at the top began to form alliances based on the manliness ethos, men in the middle did the same, though in a less spectacular fashion. Moreover, the proliferation of male

clubs, intercollegiate athletics, and the belief in practical-mind-
edness over the arts and pure science for male students is symptomatic of the direction American culture took during the final
decades of the nineteenth century. How could it be otherwise
when, according to Erik Erikson, the American boy was "faced
with a training which tended to make him machinelike and
clocklike"?[37] Yet in his later youth and manhood, he was "confronted with superior machines, complicated, incomprehensible, and impersonally dictatorial in their power to standardize
his pursuits and tastes," and if he could not maintain his autonomy, he would become a "childish joiner, or a cynical little
boss, trying to get in on some big boss' 'inside track.' "[38] Actual
machines that produced more machines thus had their coun-
terpart in social and economic machines such as bossism which
produced a class of smaller, imitative bosses.

The industrialists did not, however, dispense with the old
Jacksonian notions of character and virtue; rather, they fulfilled
them as they had never been fulfilled before or since. "To imagine that such men did not sleep the sleep of the just would be
romantic sentimentalism. In the Gilded Age even the angels sang
for them."[39] They pointed to the uncertainty of their childhood,
exalted the rags-to-riches theme in a land yielding to anyone
with an eye for the main chance, and thereby endorsed as God's
truth one of the most enduring mythologies in American life.
That mythology provided their rationalization, and they could
go about the business of creating industrial empires on an epic
scale with clear consciences. Jay Gould could say of himself and
his fellow titans that "*we* have made the country rich, *we* have
developed the country," and John D. Rockefeller could state
that "the good Lord gave me my money."[40]

Such statements, and countless others like them, were satu-
rated with the social Darwinism of Herbert Spencer, and Spencer's philosophy was, as Hofstadter has written, "admirably
suited to the American scene. It was scientific in derivation and
comprehensive in scope. It had a reassuring theory of progress
based upon biology and physics. It was large enough to be all
things to all men, broad enough to satisfy agnostics like Robert
Ingersoll and theists like Fiske and Beecher."[41] Furthermore,
social Darwinism provided an orderly means by which to re-

organize a society altered by Jacksonianism, shattered by the Civil War, and faced with Reconstruction, industrialism, economic strife, and continued westward expansion. And because Spencerian thought could be all things to all men, it was not rejected out of hand as highbrow idealism or dismissed as justifying laissez-faire economics only to entrepreneurs. Spencer was also taken as an authority by teachers, theologians, journalists, lawyers, and engineers because he managed, among other things, to instill an underlying sense of cohesiveness into a society committed to complexity. By transferring the Enlightenment belief in a regulated nature into a modern context, Spencer showed that mankind would evolve toward an orderly existence—temporary disruptions notwithstanding—if nature were allowed to take its course. Spencer thus succeeded, in John Higham's words, "where the romantics had failed: he reconciled the ideas of nature and civilization."[42]

This reconciliation of what had, during the Age of Jackson, been considered disparate concepts provided a crucial philosophical shift that helped to ease the culture away from a mood of expansiveness and into a mood of consolidation. Nature, formerly both an adversary and a temporary retreat outside civilization, became in the Gilded Age an extension of civilization to be subsumed by it and for its sake. Now men could complete the process begun by an earlier age without the attendant fears: expansion, speculation, and exploitation no longer suggested rootlessness or uncontained fluidity in a boundless land but an inevitable progress and security as the land was conquered by ever more sophisticated machines, defined by external and state boundary lines, and regulated by the economic, political, and social structures that linked East and West even as the railroad did. By the 1880s, the effects of all this ordering on the American consciousness were, as Wiebe describes them, profound:

> So great numbers of Americans came to believe that a new United States, stretched from ocean to ocean, filled out, and bound together, had miraculously appeared. That, it seemed, was the true legacy of the war, and by the early eighties publicists were savoring the word "nation" in this sense of a continent conquered and tamed. . . . An age never lent itself more readily to sweeping,

uniform description: nationalization, industrialization, mechani-
zation, urbanization.[43]

With what appeared to be prophetic accuracy, Spencer claimed
that diffusion would eventually lead to a concentration of society's best qualities as well as a nation in which men would
have a clear sense of place, purpose, and direction. As Higham
has noted, "Spencer summarized as a universal law of nature
an important shift in the culture of his time. In the United States
more than anywhere else that shift followed the Spencerian formula, circumstance that doubtless had something to do with
Spencer's great prestige here."[44] That Spencer provided the rationalization for a new era in American culture is not surprising
since he had been trained as a civil engineer, derived much of
his scientific information from hydrotechnics and population
theory, and was, all told, a product of English industrialism.
Thus, his was a system "conceived in and dedicated to an age
of steel and steam engines, competition, exploitation, and
struggle."[45]

Competition, like the getting of power and position, was, in
a male-oriented society, a means of proving who was fittest in
a struggle requiring a kind of combative, athletic prowess. Veblen, like Erikson half a century later, found evidence of the
predatory frame of mind in such things as "boys' brigades" and
other quasi-military groups, "college spirit," and intercollegiate
athletics, all of which were fostered by the adult males as means
for developing the manly character in youth:

> These manifestations of the predatory temperament are all to be
> classed under the head of exploit. They are partly simple and
> unreflected expressions of an attitude of emulative ferocity, partly
> activities deliberately entered upon with a view to gaining repute
> for prowess.... The ground of an addiction to sports is an archaic
> spiritual constitution—the possession of the predatory emulative
> propensity in a relatively high potency. A strong proclivity to
> adventuresome exploit and to the infliction of damage is especially
> pronounced in those employments which are in colloquial usage
> specifically called sportsmanship.[46]

By extending the masculinity cult's code of conduct to include the activities of boys and young men, older males could experience a vicarious return to youth—its apparent innocence and vigor—that would provide both a ceremonial reenactment of and a rationalization for what they, as battle-tested adults, were doing in their assaults on nature and the marketplace. "It is, indeed," Veblen observed, "the most noticeable effect of the sportsman's activity to keep nature in a state of chronic desolation by killing off all living things whose destruction he can compass."[47] Whether that destruction was the literal exploitation of the West or the unconscious, symbolic treatment accorded female nature, the virgin land, it was something men felt they had to do to be men. Veblen thus concludes that "in popular apprehension there is much that is admirable in the type of manhood which the life of sport fosters.... From a different point of view the qualities currently so characterized might be described as truculence and clannishness.... The traits of predatory man are by no means obsolete in the common run of modern populations."[48]

A sociologist wrote in 1896 that "it would be strange if the 'captain of the industry' did not sometimes manifest a militant spirit, for he has risen from the ranks largely because he was a better fighter than most of us. Competitive commercial life is not a flowery bed of ease, but a battlefield.... In this fierce ...contest, a peculiar type of manhood is developed, characterized by vitality, energy, concentration, skill."[49] The "battlefield" was not, however, occupied solely by the relatively few captains of industry but by an entire society that "saw its own image in the tooth-and-claw version of natural selection, and...its dominant groups were therefore able to dramatize this vision of competition as a thing good in itself. Ruthless business rivalry and unprincipled politics seemed to be justified by the survival philosophy."[50]

It is little wonder, then, that Spencer himself was a national hero and that his visit to the United States in 1882 prompted the ceremony and passionate rhetoric accorded heads of state. The popularity of his philosophy, according to Cochran and Miller, rested on the fact that it was flexible enough to support businessmen in whatever they wanted to do: "When they were hopeful, it was infinitely optimistic; when they were harsh, it 'proved' that harshness was the only road to progress; when they had doubts, it allayed these with a show of evidence that apparently was irrefutable. Their cupidity, it defended as part of the universal struggle for existence; their wealth, it hallowed as the sign of the 'fittest.' Business America in the Gilded Age had supreme faith in itself; no wonder it embraced Spencer's philosophy, which sanctified business activities."[51] And tycoons were some of Spencer's most devoted disciples. Rockefeller, for instance, claimed that "growth of a large business is merely a survival of the fittest." James J. Hill believed "the fortunes of railroad companies are determined by the law of the survival of the fittest," and George Hearst stated that "I have travelled a good deal and observed men and things and I have made up my mind after all my experience that the members of the Senate are the survivors of the fittest."[52]

Theirs was a fitness of a particular kind, however, and while it is true that the barons of business saw themselves as the fittest among human beings in general, it is even more to the point that they saw themselves as the fittest among men in particular. They did not merely survive, they survived and flourished by controlling other men and using whatever means necessary to do so, including bribery, spying, threats, exploitation of workers, and dynamiting the property of competitors.[53] John Jacob Astor manipulated Indians with whiskey, made a fortune in furs, and invested so much money in eastern land and banks that his heir, William B. Astor, was called "the landlord of New York." "Commodore" Cornelius Vanderbilt, who began as an illiterate ferry-boy, became a living definition of a captain of industry with his accumulations in shipping, railroads, iron, and steel. His tactic was to snuff out the competition with low rates, then raise them and never let go. Massive control over the economic system thus became, under the aegis of free enterprise, the way to wealth and, therefore, the way to self-importance for men equal to the task. In short, great management signified great prowess.

Wasserstrom, for instance, claims that "the pursuit of wealth, conceived as the most telling evidence of human uniqueness, importance, individuality, was in effect the most convincing sign of malehood. This idea was reinforced by the growing conviction that the genteel ideal may have assured virtue but, dissipating desire, it also suffocated zeal—the urge to build, to transform the wilderness, to create."[54] It follows, then, that those like Dreiser's Frank Cowperwood, who broke through the moral suffocation, who rechanneled dissipated desire to other ends, were not only the most successful but the manliest of men. The rite of passage for these men, most of whom came of age around the time of the Civil War, was neither sexual nor social but economic, and to prove themselves they subdued the land, establishing their monetary—i.e., manly—independence by making others dependent on them.

Much of the wealth in the nineteenth century was tied to the land, on it or beneath it, and the anxious, economically motivated male turned to nature not for subsistence but for spoils, asserting his masculinity either by plundering the resources of the East or forcing the frontier into submission. As Michael Rogin points out, land had meaning in nineteenth-century America unlike anything before or since:

> Land had not only symbolic value and use value, but exchange value as well. It was...available to be exploited, bought, and sold. At bottom the two meanings of the land shared common roots. They were joined, first, by primitiveness. The land lacked, or had been stripped of, specific historical memories; it provided space to act out fantasies of total sustenance, great fortune, and omnipotent control. Second, the economic importance of the land sustained its spiritual meaning. Glorification of the virgin land did not float in an empyrean realm, irrelevant to daily American business. Nature gave higher meaning to dreams of future fortune; it sanctified the frenetic quest for wealth, and offered promise of bliss at the end of the road.[55]

Nature, once the retreat for such literary and folk heroes as Bumppo and Boone, became by mid-century a violent stage for the American who, threatened by democracy and an effeminate East, played out one of the most tragic dramas of the century. The history of the development of California after 1849 supplies a microcosm of the tragedy, one repeated wherever nature had not yet been settled, urbanized, and managed by commerce and industry. Unlike the ideal Jeffersonian yeoman living in a state of suspended animation between primitivism and industrialism

or unlike the Jacksonians who feared civilization's authority over
them, neo-Jacksonian sons and grandsons took action against
the land in the name of civilization, a phenomenon Stanley Diamond uses to distinguish between the integrated personality of
primitive man and the neurotic behavior of modern man. He
observes of the latter that

> the power of the 'owners' or chief executives became an inhuman
> power. But their freedom is a pseudo-freedom, for it is based on
> the coercion of subordinate groups; they are bound to those whom
> they exploit. Their social ties grow manipulative; their privi-
> leges—irresponsible. Nor do the managers, technicians, bureau-
> crats and clerks escape this fate. It is the present agony and peril
> of all classes and grades in a civilized society. If civilized pro-
> duction has helped disorganize modern man and deprive him of
> his moral center, primitive production helped to integrate pri-
> mitive man.[56]

Yet Diamond's thesis—that to save ourselves we must return
to the primitive—is finally untenable. Or it has not worked.
Rather than returning to the primitive, integrated life, civilized
men took their neuroses with them and became predatory. Veblen and Erikson have said as much, and the conclusion is clear:
the neuroses run too deep to be shed. Nineteenth-century man
moved into the primitive land and among its people not to re-
discover his elemental self, but to redefine himself in terms of
exploitative prowess and thereby establish the criteria for success
in a civilized society and for the progress of the race. The "Indian
question," for example, first confronted as a serious national
issue during the Age of Jackson, was settled once and for all by
white men in post-bellum America. To them, the Indians lived
in a perpetual state of childhood with nature their mother, and
they were, therefore, destined to succumb to whites whose righteousness was based on the biblical mandate to subdue and
replenish the earth as well as the cultural faith in Manifest Destiny, which, after the Mexican War, became a doctrine of domestic imperialism. Thus, while the Indians were considered
members of the human family, even older brothers in the wilderness, it was felt that they were children who would never
grow up. They had to be subdued and confined because "their

replacement by whites symbolized America's growing up from childhood to maturity,"[57] which is to say, the killing of Indians was a symbolic rejection of one's own childhood, a disassociation from female nature, the great mother of all men. Moreover, according to Winthrop Jordan, fighting the Indian "was a testing experience.... Conquering the Indian symbolized and personified the conquest of American difficulties, the surmounting of the wilderness. To push back the Indian was to prove the worth of one's own mission, to make straight in the desert a highway for civilization."[58] Although Jordan's study focuses on an earlier period in American history, the principle he sets forth is perhaps even more valid for the decades immediately before and after the Civil War when the nation had both the machinery and the manpower to complete the task. Thus, those Indians who resisted were slain while the rest were eventually confined to reservations where the white agents—managers of another kind—could control them. And with revealing metaphors, *The United States Magazine and Democratic Review* expressed the inevitable necessity of an assault on nature by white civilization:

> A wolf and a lamb are not more antagonistical in the system of organic beings, than are civilization and barbarism.... Civilization may be likened to an absorbent body, placed in contact with an antiabsorbent, for some of the properties of which it has strong affinities. It will draw these latter so completely out, that, to use a strong phrase, it may be said to eat them up.[59]

The wolf, a tenacious, masculine figure, must consume the lamb, a passive, female figure, and according to Leslie Fiedler, cultural myths concerning the Indian, nature, and women depended on what the WASP male perceived as he looked first one way, then the other, from his position in the clearing. And what he saw in the Indian was not what he saw in the black. The Indian threat rose from the pre-sexual, childhood stage of development—a mixture of indolence and insane aggression—rather than from the sexual, oedipal stage, and the red man, therefore, had to be suppressed or destroyed so that the white man could grow up.[60] The red man and the wilderness, a mothering nature, had to be defeated so that, in Rogin's words, "by killing Indians, whites grounded their growing up in a securely achieved manhood, and securely possessed their land."[61]

As quoted earlier, Leo Marx maintains that while contact with the wilderness may strip away the facades of civilization, what allows men to return to nature at all is the knowledge that such an adventure is only temporary. It is a round trip into the primitive and back again.[62] Thus, in pathetic irony, nature was not only a refuge for wildlife but an adversary to be beaten as a test of manliness over immense odds. Money, power, and, therefore, a sense of manliness, awaited those willing to assert themselves, and western enticements such as the following were common in newspapers of the time:

> Prosperity, Independence, Freedom, Manhood in its highest sense, peace of mind and all the comforts and luxuries of life are awaiting you.... Throw down the yardstick and come out here if you would be men. Bid good-by to the theater and turn your backs on the crowd in the street![63]

The ironies thicken. To gain their freedom and their manly independence, men moved westward en masse, using and promoting the latest technological innovations from the East and forming a masculine alliance in order to subdue a weaker, often passive, nature with a combination of overwhelming numbers, advanced weaponry, and the greatest machine of the age, the railroad.

The two frontiers of the nineteenth century—business and the actual land—merged in the westward movement, and like the East, the West had its symbolic, masculine prototypes who stirred the popular imagination and kept men up and doing. In particular, the Pacific Association formed by Collis Huntington, Mark Hopkins, Leland Stanford, and Charles Crocker was a group of pioneering businessmen who manipulated the money and political power necessary to finance the Central Pacific Railroad and its connection with the eastern Union Pacific in 1869. It was a symbolic merger of East and West, the men who backed it, and the values they represented to a nation enamored with the cult of progress and the doctrine of Manifest Destiny. Secretive and paranoid, the Pacific Association was dominated by Hun-

tington and Stanford, an "aggressive figure of 'virile power,' "
and "if the four men ever quarreled, out of jealousy or mutual
fear, their dissension was kept silent; they bore their consciences
in common, kept each other's secrets and preserved an unbroken
discipline against the common enemy, wherever he might be."[64]

By dominating the railroad systems of the entire West Coast,
the Pacific Associates were able to expand their financial empire
with land holdings, iron and coal mines, shipping, and payroll
politicians until, by the last decade of the century, they had
formed alliances with the major industrial circles in the East.
Among others, Gould and Carnegie in steel and Rockfeller's
Standard Oil became their allies. As one member of the Association wrote to Huntington in 1878, "I have learned one thing,
we have got no true friends outside of us five. We cannot depend
on a human soul outside of ourselves, and hence we must all
be good-natured, stick together and keep our own counsels."[65]
To the east, the merger of Andrew Carnegie's steel operation
with Henry Clay Frick's in coke in 1883 produced a similar clan-
destine machine called Carnegie Associates while Rockefeller's
conglomerate was bound together with the cultism of a fraternal
organization which, indeed, it was:

> Those who came in were promised wealth beyond their dreams.
> The remarkable economies and profits of the Standard were ex-
> posed to their eyes. "We mean to secure the entire refining busi-
> ness of the world," they were told. They were urged to dissemble
> their actions. Contracts were entered into with the peculiar secret
> rites which Mr. Rockefeller habitually preferred. They were signed
> late at night at his Euclid Avenue home in Cleveland. The par-
> ticipants were besought not to tell even their wives about the
> new arrangements, to conceal the gains they made, not to drive
> fast horses or put on style, or buy new bonnets, or do anything
> to let people suspect there were unusual profits in oil-refining,
> since that might invite competition.[66]

These were constricted, tightly managed groups of hard-bitten,
cynical men who operated in a womanless world and who devised intricate systems as stays against disruption.

Masculine alliances, with chapters in the East and the West,
achieved a union of Pacific and Atlantic with belts of commerce

along each with which to circumscribe nature and to cinch their images as prophets of progress. Other men, less skilled or less ruthless, gave these prophets their due if only because in the Gilded Age, as in the Age of Jackson, cultural symbols and heroes were needed to corroborate current thought. And in Huntington, Stanford, Gould, Carnegie, Rockefeller, and the like, it was apparent that the fittest had survived and that the great managers had made of themselves something which no amount of education, culture, or idle refinement could produce. Prowess was demonstrated through power, virtue through virility; and both power and virility were made visible through the machines—literal and metaphorical—which did the work. Thus, a statue of Commodore Vanderbilt on Hudson Street in New York was flanked on either side by sailing vessels, war ships, steamboats, railroad bridges, locomotives, and passenger cars, and Mayor Oakey Hall of the Tweed ring described him as "a remarkable prototype of the rough-hewn American character which can carve the way of every humbly-born boy to national eminence."[67] So long as "every humbly-born boy" believed his claim, statues such as this one were cultural icons for an age.

Along similar lines, Thomas C. Cochran attempts to correct the "historical mythology" that renders the robber barons as evil or "unusually grasping and unscrupulous types in our culture against the background of a 'good' public."[68] They were not, in other words, aberrations but ultimate manifestations of the validity of such cultural themes as a self-adjusting, autonomous economy, progress through survival of the fittest, and the belief that profit was the only reliable reason for action. As Cochran has put it, "The truckman delivering dirt for railroad construction was as much motivated by profit and as firm a believer in these themes as was the 'robber baron' who was building the road."[69] And Veblen has observed that the captain of industry "was one of the major institutions of the nineteenth century, and as such he has left his mark on the culture of that time and after, in other bearings as well as in the standards of business enterprise.... The Captain of Industry and his work in interests presently became the focus of attention and deference. The Landed Interest, the political buccaneers, and the priesthood, yielded him the first place in affairs and in the councils of the nation, civil and political."[70]

The inheritors of the Jacksonian legacy never looked back. Erikson represents these free sons with a prototypical adolescent who, bewildered by his machine-like training and his freedom to develop himself in any direction, "feels so rich in his opportunities for free expression that he often no longer knows what it is he is free from. Neither does he know where he is not free; he does not recognize his native autocrats when he sees them. He is too immediately occupied with being efficient and being decent."[71] If, therefore, the middle class did not consciously emulate the Vanderbilts, the Rockefellers, the Carnegies, and the Morgans, it did so unconsciously by permitting their excesses to go unchecked due to a preoccupation with prosperity and order that shielded the business and political machines from view. A locomotive could be seen, a monopoly could not, even though one symbolized the other, as Leo Marx has shown, with a masculine, ruthless will to conquer.[72] And the middle class, misjudging the symbols of the age and acting on the emotional appeal they generated, pursued success and progress with Spencerian devotion.

Money and prowess, as Veblen understood them, were inextricably linked so that "in order to stand well in the eyes of the community, it is necessary to come up to a certain, somewhat indefinite, conventional standard of wealth; just as in the earlier predatory state it is necessary for the barbarian man to come up to the tribe's standard of physical endurance, cunning and skill at arms. A certain standard of wealth in one case, and of prowess in the other, is a necessary condition of reputability, and anything in excess of this normal amount is meritorious."[73] The barons and bosses may have relied on middle class indifference and naivete to fulfill the culture's values to the extreme but to be true manifestations of American culture, those values also had to have been an integral part of middle class ideology, which is to say, middle class male ideology. In his description of the typical young male, Erikson suggests that he will be an efficient, moral, industrious type who enjoys taking his recreation with "the boys." In short, he is the product of American education, formal and cultural, and along with others of his kind, represents the strength of the nation.[74]

There was, however, an education of another kind, the one chronicled by Henry Adams in his autobiographical *The Education of Henry Adams*. He, too, was a son of the Age of Jackson, though also a victim of it since the Adams dynasty had fallen to the Jacksonian mystique. Yet precisely because he was, in a sense, detached from the mainstream of the culture by his training and his aristocratic New England blood, Adams reacted differently from most Americans to the symbols of the time. The crucial event for him was his visit to the Paris Exposition of 1900 where, confronted with great mechanical devices and the concept of force, "he found himself lying in the Gallery of Machines...his historical neck broken by the sudden irruption of forces totally new."[75] Those forces were embodied in the Dynamo and the Virgin, and the clash between them was to be seen in an industrialized society threatening to destroy the creative power that Adams believed to be responsible for most of the good, and the beautiful, in human history.

Adams, whose life covered the development of the railroad, saw at the end of the century that the machine had come of age and that its energy was the composite of a nation's since it had denied the power of Eros for the power of the Dynamo:

> This problem in dynamics gravely perplexed an American historian. The Woman had once been supreme; in France she still seemed potent, not merely as a sentiment, but as a force. Why was she unknown in America? For evidently America was ashamed of her, and she was ashamed of herself, otherwise they would not have strewn fig-leaves so profusely all over her. When she was a true force, she was ignorant of fig-leaves, but the monthly-magazine-made American female had not a feature that would have been recognized by Adam. The trait was notorious, and often humorous, but any one brought up among Puritans knew that sex was sin. In any previous age, sex was strength.[76]

While Adams's assessment of Puritan attitudes toward sex is inaccurate, or at least incomplete, he makes his point nonetheless. In repressing the forces of spiritual and sexual love, Americans had turned to machines for whatever creative power they needed and for the gods they chose to worship. Adams was confronted with the horrifying realization that nineteenth-century Americans had directed their love into what he perceived as instruments of destruction rather than enduring works of art capable of preserving the humanness of the race. "His Dynamo," Leo Marx has written, "is the modern force most nearly equivalent, in its command over human behavior, to the sublimated sexual vitality that built Chartres."[77] The difference is that the sublimation that created Chartres was, for Adams at least, positive, an expression and celebration of love, while the sublimation that created and wielded the machine was negative, a confirmation of brute power and the passion for money Tocqueville had observed in Americans even before Adams was born.

Adams's lament over the triumph of technology reveals his own peculiar brand of cynicism through which he sifts his perceptions and at least partially misjudges events. Is it possible, for instance, to deny the advantages of building cathedrals, or anything else, with machines rather than with the blood and sweat of the poor? Likewise, is it possible to deny that technology has produced good as well as bad effects for society? Yet despite his embittered and exaggerated reaction, Adams did recognize a major phenomenon in nineteenth-century American life, one that saw Jacksonianism fulfilled in the Gilded Age and the entrepreneur prove what men could accomplish when left to themselves and their own devices. In an attempt to contain the fluid chaos of an earlier time, men first restricted their energy, then channeled it into the pursuit of wealth and the management of great machines. As a Frenchman observed, the typical American does, after all, have "a perfect passion for railroads; he loves them . . . as a lover loves his mistress."[78]

4

HE-MAN MAGAZINES AND THE AMERICAN SUPER-MALE: A CASE STUDY IN TWENTIETH-CENTURY POPULAR CULTURE

Looking at history, like glancing back through a window at the long road that brought us home, we see, when the light is just so, not only where we came from but ourselves as well. The road leads to us, moves through us, and in this fusion of images we perceive the past for what it is—at once something "back there" and the process of our becoming. Thus, modern evidence of the masculinity cult in American life appears in the works of Hemingway, West, Faulkner, Mailer, and Kesey, to name but a few well-known writers, and in the proliferation of he-man magazines flooding the market. Yet the fact that these authors have achieved academic respectability suggests that their primary importance is literary rather than cultural in the broader sense of the term. By contrast, the heroes and heroic stories of he-man magazines provide clues to the character of the men who read them, to the nature of their culture, and to the ways in which they perceive the world. Richard Slotkin, for instance, recalls "Davy Crockett grinning by a mountain of 105 bear-hides" and "Boone, whose rifle shots are prayer and poetry."[1] These are men whose legendary exploits remain lodged in the American male's consciousness. "The heroism in these figures," Slotkin states, "consists for us in their method of achieving their goal. The trophies they are perpetually garnering have no material value; their sanctity derives from their function as visual and concrete proofs of the self-justifying acts of violent self-transcendence and regeneration that produced them. . . .In Vietnam it was called the body count."[2] Since heroism, or manliness, is often gauged indirectly, or symbolically, certain principles of psychology are necessary for an understanding of the manliness ethos in modern America. And as John G. Cawelti has pointed out in his important book, *The Six-Gun Mystique*, two Freudian concepts have dominated discussions of the psychological properties of art in the twentieth century: first, art arises from some psychic conflict which seeks resolution in symbols and fantasy; and, secondly, art vicariously satisfies deeply felt impulses which cannot be fulfilled in daily life (i.e., wish fulfillment).[3] Both of these concepts are helpful in assessing he-man literature and, therefore, the motivations of the men who read it.

Cawelti, like Slotkin, has found the justification of violence to be one of the major themes of western stories. That is, adversaries are rendered in such a way that the hero is morally and emotionally justified in destroying them, and the narrative thus resolves "the tension between a strong need for aggression and a sense of ambiguity and guilt about violence."[4] Cawelti's analysis of the Western in these terms would also seem to hold for he-man stories in general—based as so many of them are on various forms of violence—and his findings concerning the audience for the Western are equally applicable here, too:

> He would expect to find the compulsion to encounter and seek a resolution for this tension to be strongest among male adolescents. But. . .there are social-psychological reasons why this kind of tension also exists among lower middle and working class males, for in modern industrial societies, these groups are constantly subjected to the pressures of social change in such a way that their sense of masculine independence is continuously threatened. For blue-collar and white-collar workers at the lower echelons of the large industrial organization. . .the corporation plays somewhat the same psychological role as the father does for the adolescent boy; it is recognized as an inescapable authority upon whose benevolence the individual is dependent, yet at the same

time, it is an object of the most violent hostility and a basic threat to the individual's ego.[5]

Cawelti's view of the corporation as a father-figure is a variation of the psychohistorical theory that the father-figure, rejected during the American Revolution, reemerged late in the nineteenth century as a bad father—e.g., the robber baron—and he has continued to be a fixation for the modern male through such figures as the political boss, the corrupt union leader, and the gangster. Cawelti's assessment suggests, therefore, why a significant portion of American men read he-man literature. That is, it provides an important psychological function by vicariously satisfying the long-held urge among some males to assert their masculine dominance, "long held" because the psychological makeup of the modern he-man is based largely on nineteenth-century prototypes. He is the twentieth-century repository of an impulse that arose out of Jacksonian egalitarianism to produce a powerful class of men at the top as models for the masses in the Gilded Age, and he thus completes a percolating effect in the culture by emulating the virtues they associated with virility.

Like his nineteenth-century predecessors, today's he-man possesses a predatory temperament, the manifestations of which are, according to Thorstein Veblen, "to be classed under the head of exploit. They are partly simple and unreflected expressions of an attitude of emulative ferocity, partly activities deliberately entered upon with a view to gaining repute for prowess."[6] Veblen further explains this process of emulation in his observation that "in modern civilized communities the lines of demarcation between social classes have grown vague and transient, and wherever this happens the norm of reputability imposed by the upper class extends to the lowest strata. The result is that the members of each stratum accept as their ideal of decency the scheme of life in vogue in the next higher stratum, and bend their energies to live up to that ideal."[7] And for the masculinity cult in contemporary America, that ideal draws upon the manliness ethos as it was developed and expressed in the nineteenth century.

When, therefore, the modern he-man empathizes with, or emulates, heroic figures of the past, he is choosing those men

whose characteristics, real or mythical, embody a powerful virility: Andrew Jackson, for one, and Theodore Roosevelt, for
another. Both of these men were mythical military heroes; both
were given familiar nicknames ("Old Hickory" and "Teddy"
respectively); and both masked an aristocratic orientation beneath an exterior of rough-hewn ways. It was Roosevelt, for
instance, who claimed that hunting in the West represents "the
free, self-reliant, adventurous life" and that stalking game en-
courages a "vigorous manliness for the lack of which in a nation,
as in an individual, the possession of no other qualities can
possibly atone." Moreover, Roosevelt found much to admire in
leaders such as Jackson and Lincoln because "they hunted much
in their youth, if only as an incident in the prolonged warfare
waged by themselves and their kinsmen against the wild forces
of nature."[8] In this regard, Roosevelt, a major national figure
around the turn of the century, was an amalgamation of nineteenth-century attitudes—Jacksonian as well as post-bellum—
because nature was not only a hostile force to be defeated as a
test of manliness, it was a "wild" force to be contained. He was,
then, a pivotal figure, or link, between the real frontier and the
mythologized frontier of the modern era, the popularized version of his character—a civilized cowboy—sanctioning he-man
behavior in this century. As Edward G. White has written, in
Roosevelt "the love of the outdoors...evolved into a cult of
manliness with all its trimmings—aggressiveness, belligerency,
belief in 'hardihood' as a 'fundamental virtue'—that seemed to
be enjoyed largely for its own sake."[9] Yet traits that appear to
be their own rewards often run much deeper in their significance, and Roosevelt's self-conscious masculinity suggests a great
deal about modern American males who nostalgically try to define themselves in terms of the past even as they are firmly
committed to the present.

Magazines such as *True, Climax, Male, Stag, Argosy*, and *Saga*
do not imply or merely suggest the existence of a masculinity
cult in American life; they are some of the chief documents of
the cult, bought and read by men whose values and ideas are
shaped by an obsessive virility. The resulting super-male point
of view is rooted in the past, especially the Old West, and certain

rituals of manhood reenacting those traditions inherited from
our mythologized frontier experience:

> A ritual is a means of reaffirming certain basic cultural values,
> resolving tensions and establishing a sense of continuity between
> present and past. The Western, with its historical setting, its
> thematic emphasis on the establishment of law and order, and
> its resolution of the conflict between civilization and savagery on
> the frontier, is a kind of foundation ritual. It presents for our
> renewed contemplation that epic moment when the frontier passed
> from the old way of life into social and cultural forms directly
> connected with the present.[10]

For the American male, however, other tensions exist besides
those between the past and the present, or between the call of
the wild and civilization. In *Childhood and Society*, Erik Erikson
maintains that the frontier created a society wherein "Mom"—
a stereotyped caricature expressing the contradictions created
by intense and as yet unassimilated historical change—found
that it was her task to set up new patterns of sedentary life in
a country populated by men whose original motive for immi-
grating to America was to avoid, in one way or another, being
"fenced in."[11] Furthermore, those men did not leave their fear
of confinement behind them when they came to America—the
whole westward movement implies as much—and although, as
Erikson suggests, women had "to become autocratic in their
demands for some order,"[12] it must be remembered that the
relationship between the sexes in the nineteenth century was a
tacit bargain struck by men and women for mutual security and
self-identity. And in the chaotic world of men's affairs, women
supplied what men could not provide for themselves, and
"Mom," still circumscribed but given a definite, nonheterosexual
part to play, became an institution in American life.

Yet her femaleness and what was perceived as her incessant
efforts to infiltrate the male world outside the home continue to
haunt and to threaten men who have been regrouping and attempting to preserve their traditional bastions of manliness ever
since the frontier closed and women were enfranchised. This
perennial anxiety over female encroachments on male prerog-

atives does not manifest itself directly so often as indirectly, through the projection, or displacement, of the anxiety onto others. In an advertisement for itself, *True* declares that

> one word describes the new TRUE magazine: MACHO. The honest-to-God American MAN deserves a magazine sans naked cuties, Dr. Spock philosophies, foppish, gutless "unisex" pap, and platform shoes. It's time for a refreshing change. . . . A hardy slice of adventure, challenge, action, competition, controversy. Including informative features that bring the American man and American values back from the shadows. Back from the sterile couches of pedantic psychiatrists. Back from behind the frivolous skirts of libbers. . . . If you're a man, you'll like it.[13]

By *True*'s own admission, the American male is in the shadows— i.e., a blurred sense of his own psychosexual identity—and his only way out is to reject effeminate influences on the culture in favor of a life of action and adventure. With the exception of "libbers" (whose womanliness would be questioned anyway), *True* does not reject females *per se*, and the readers of this magazine, like others of its kind, thus achieve their independence from women indirectly and vicariously.

Other magazines define the he-man with similar candor. Beneath a photograph of John Wayne in his western costume and with his arm around Norman Rockwell's shoulders, the publisher of *Argosy* records his tribute to one of the most durable heroes of the modern masculinity cult:

> So it is that we were privileged to have the most famous illustrator of the 20th century, Norman Rockwell, paint those familiar, rough-hewn features of our cover subject, John Wayne. (Rockwell's painting is now on permanent display at the Cowboy Hall of Fame in Oklahoma City, Oklahoma.) Rockwell, after meeting the famous "Duke" for the first time, observed: "He's the most mannish man I've ever met." Millions of theater-goers feel the same way.[14]

In addition, Rockwell is shown wearing a sport coat and smoking a pipe, yet he cradles a six-shooter in his hands: a merger of the modern man and the cowboy in Rockwell and Wayne first, then in Rockwell himself. This merger, or at least its attempt, lies at the center of the he-man philosophy and gathered about it are the popular concepts of the American West.

At an early age, boys play at being cowboys and the adult, really a boy-man, continues to reenact this role not as a fantasy but as an integral part of his personal identity. It was F. Scott Fitzgerald who wrote that "there are no second acts in American lives"[15] and concerning the he-man's extended belief in western models from childhood to adulthood, Fitzgerald's assertion seems apt. The super-male accepts as valid what was once an entertaining illusion of childhood. Yet precisely what he accepts is more complex than role-playing simply converted into a lifestyle because a system of values is involved, values arising not so much from what the original cowboy was but rather from what the modern he-man believes him to have been.

The advocate of the manliness ethos is a hunter of one kind or another. He may fish or stalk his prey with bow and arrow (an ironic impersonation given the white man's traditional hatred and fear of the red man), but most often he hunts with a gun. This recurring journey into the wilderness provides the middle stage between childhood western games and adult he-manhood. That is, hunting permits the father to teach the boy the difference between toy guns and real guns, between play killing and real killing, between fantasized survival and actual life or death. Thus, what was at one time a necessity—the frontiersman supplying food for his family by hunting—has, in the twentieth century, become a ritual, a rite of passage for future he-men. Slotkin explains the mytho-historical significance of the hunt:

> Believing in the myth of regeneration through the violence of the hunt, the American hunters eventually destroyed the natural conditions that had made possible their economic and social freedom, their democracy of social mobility. Yet the mythology and the value system it supported remained even after the objective conditions that had justified it had vanished.[16]

According to Slotkin, Americans have never stopped associating democracy and progress with endless social mobility—both vertical and horizontal—and thus "our economic, social, and spiritual life is taken to be a series of initiations, of stages in a movement outward and upward toward some transcendent goal. We have traditionally associated this form of aspiring initiation with the self-transcendence achieved by hunters through acts of predation."[17] The wilderness and civilization—the two force fields between which the hunter constantly moves—alternate as adversaries for the hunter to defeat and, therefore, to transcend.

Hunting on the frontier often involved more than killing just for food since the West was not merely opened, it was ripped apart by those who slaughtered the Indian, the Mexican, the Oriental, not to mention the seal, the beaver, and the buffalo. Facts such as these corroborate Veblen's observation that the most apparent effect of sportsmen's activities is "to keep nature in a state of chronic desolation by killing off all living things whose destruction he can compass," and he concludes that "the traits of predatory man are by no means obsolete in the common run of modern populations."[18] Yet historical facts are often excluded from the frontier tradition retained by today's he-man, and this makes him a curiously ahistorical student of the past, one who inherits and passes on neither the frontiersman's methods nor actual experience but his mystique based on an emotional longing for the good old days, on the displacement of an idea. The horse, the bedroll, and the attendant difficulties of survival in the wilderness have been replaced by the four-wheel-drive vehicle and elaborate gear, many times including a camper or trailer for protection from the very wilderness the he-man wishes to engage. The real moment of manly truth, though, comes with the kill, as a high-powered rifle explodes and the animal drops. The impersonal, long-distance kill eliminates any risk of confrontation between man and beast even as it assuages any guilt associated with killing. Therefore, the hours or even days of drudgery spent moving in and moving out are instantly justified with little or no peril, and manliness—i.e., its ritualized, historical equivalent—is either confirmed in the boy or reaffirmed in the adult. In addition, women and children have been reassured against any invisible threats "out there" by the man's successful trek into and return from the wilderness, a region where not only fierce animals used to roam but Indians and immigrants as well. Thus returning to home and civilization, the hunter often exhibits the symbolic proof of his masculinity—antlers, a head, or even an entire animal stuffed—as a reminder to his family and to other men long after the meat has been eaten.

The he-man as hunter suggests a reversed Natty Bumppo figure who, to be sure, needs the wilderness though not for solace or communion with God but as a proving ground. For Cooper's hero, slaughter was repulsive; for the prototypical male, it is mandatory. Nature is hostile, something to be subdued rather than absorbed, and the he-man places himself in the role of the solitary hero who confronts just enough ruggedness and peril to make the struggle for survival convincing to himself and others. In "Buck in the Hills," a story by Walter Van Tilburg Clark in *Climax*, the narrator recounts his partner's brutal slaying of a deer, how he wounded it intentionally then tracked it until it collapsed so he could slit its throat. The story ends with the hunters' departing from the forest while sensing nature's hostility toward them and their bloody intrusion:

> We packed up and went back down the trail, single file and not talking. Snow makes a hush that's even harder to talk in than the clear silence. There was something listening behind each tree and rock we passed, and something waiting among the taller trees down the slope, blue through the falling snow. They wouldn't stop us, but they didn't like us, either. The snow was their ally.[19]

Thus, while both Natty Bumppo and the modern he-man define themselves according to their relationship with nature, the pantheistic awe of Cooper's character has become, in the modern deerslayer, an uneasiness so intense that it smacks of paranoia. And though he may be a member of a hunting party, he is nonetheless alone because solipsism, too, is a part of the frontier experience he has ritualized.

In *Virgin Land*, Henry Nash Smith discusses the mountain man and Kit Carson in terms similar to those used here in dealing with the modern he-man:

> The Wild Western hero has been secularized—if the term may be employed in this connection—and magnified. He no longer looks to God through nature, for nature is no longer benign; its symbols

are the wolves and the prairie fire. The scene has been shifted from the deep fertile forests east of the Mississippi to the barren plains. The landscape within which the Western hero operates has become, in Averill's words, a "dreary waste." It throws the hero back in upon himself and accentuates his terrible and sublime isolation. He is an anarchic and self-contained atom—hardly even a monad—alone in a hostile, or at best a neutral, universe.[20]

Smith's depiction of the western hero is similar to Matthew Josephson's assessment of the kings of commerce, and together they suggest a connection between the alienated frontiersman and the isolated businessman at the top:

> The truth is that once arrived in the metropolis of fastidious luxury, installed at last in the palace of Dives, the nobility of American business seemed bored, bewildered, lost. The excitement of empire building and destroying had gripped them like a powerful drug, so long as it had lasted; but it had not prepared them in any sense for an art of leisure, or for cultivated intercourse with each other....Few of them knew how to talk, or knew what to do with themselves.[21]

Concerning the myth of the nineteenth-century isolato, Slotkin has written that "under the aspect of mythology and historical distance, the acts and motives of the woodchopper, the whale and bear hunter, the Indian fighter, and the deerslayer have an air of simplicity and purity that makes them seem finely heroic expressions of an admirable quality of the human spirit. They seem to stand on a commanding ridge, while we are still tangled in the complexities of the world and the wilderness. But their apparent independence of time and consequence is an illusion; a closely woven chain of time and consequence binds their world to ours."[22] Thus, like the historical characters he venerates, the he-man moves brusquely, often violently, across the land and bristles at those unlike himself in order to define, through acts of prowess, who he is in a complex world. For him, manliness still involves—as he believes it did a century or more ago—the willingness to act alone against nature, to spurn for at least a while the niceties of civilized life, and to thump his chest at those who, different from himself, would cast aspersion on his manly ways.

The isolato pitted against either the actual frontier or the wilderness of daily life indicates another, related characteristic of the masculinity cult, for if he is alone, he carries with him a strong sense of his aloneness, self-imposed and necessary. If he makes it as a man, he must do so by himself; the virtues of manliness cannot be realized any other way. An article on "The Cowboy Hall of Fame" in *Argosy* expresses this tenet of he-manism:

> Such outspoken individualism characterizes the men surrounding the Hall. "We're free and independent, just like the Old West," fiercely proud Krakel [founder of the Cowboy Hall of Fame] can afford to say today. "We're not beholden to anybody. There's no government money in the Hall of Fame. We're prouder of that than anything else. Our individualism is what made this country great, just like the rodeo, where the riders put up their own money. They have no coaches, no NFL-type unions, no doctor, no frills. You're on your own. And so are we!"[23]

What *Argosy* fails to perceive, of course, is that the rodeo is not the Old West or even an accurate replica of it but rather a highly stylized ritualization of the western tradition: horsemanship, roping, covered wagon races, yelling and firing blank bullets into the air, and so on. The modern rodeo—faithful to Buffalo Bill's Wild West Show, which began after the frontier was declared closed—makes the Old West a form of entertainment focusing on the cowboy who, once again, must single-handedly subdue various representatives of malevolent nature: the wild bull to be ridden, the steer to be wrestled to the ground, the bucking bronco to be broken. Similarly, the he-man magazine descends from another form of popular literature in the nineteenth century, the dime novel, and the heroes of each share much in common. The above passage from *Argosy*, for instance, parallels Smith's description of Deadwood Dick and the dime novel in general:

> The most important traits of Deadwood Dick are that he too is without the upper-class rank which belongs exclusively to East-

erners or Englishmen; that he possesses to a high degree such
characteristic skills as riding and shooting....Deadwood Dick
fully illustrates the principle that Merle Curti found to be central
in the dime novel. Overcoming his enemies by his own efforts
and courage, he embodies the popular ideal of the self-made
man.[24]

Yet the he-man magazine's concept of the masculine male—
a blend of hunter, cowboy, and self-made man—creates a dilemma for those who subscribe to it, because if he is a loner
then he is also an outsider who can neither rejoin his mythologized past nor fully accept his own modernism in rejection of
that past. Buffalo Bill, Smith points out, has been quoted as
saying of himself that he "stood between savagery and civilization most all my early days,"[25] and this describes the twentieth-century he-man, too. Thus, unlike Natty Bumppo who
sought a total immersion in nature, today's he-man moves back
and forth between two worlds, needing both because he is fulfilled by neither. He is, perhaps, the final product of the tran-
sitional movement in literature from Bumppo, in harmony with
his environment, to those characters whose lives are spent going
out and coming back—Rip Van Winkle, for instance, Ishmael,
or Huck Finn—until, in this century, the he-man is often no
more heroic than Sinclair Lewis's George Babbitt who periodically flees to the masculine world of Maine's forests or, in a
related context, Hemingway's Francis Macomber who achieves
momentary manliness by facing the wounded water buffalo.
From Bumppo to Babbitt and beyond, including the virile characters of popular magazines, these men flee from women and
into a female nature they face as an adversary. Slotkin further
illuminates this phenomenon of incessant motion by placing it
in a psychosocial context reminiscent of Jacksonian animosity
toward the monied aristocracy:

> In a democracy based on the social equality of the upwardly
> mobile, perpetual motion is as important a sign of social impor-
> tance as the possession of an established fortune. Indeed, the
> former is of more value, since stagnant or inherited wealth is, by
> the hunter's standards, a sign of lost vigor. The myth of the
> hunter...is one of self-renewal or self-creation through acts of

violence. What becomes of the new self, once the initiatory hunt is over? If the good life is defined in terms of the hunter myth, there is only another hunt succeeding the first one. Thus Boone ultimately departs from Boonesborough, the cycles of departure and return continuing beyond the conclusion of the first....Crockett, having failed in Tennessee, hunts for new animals, new enemies...only to die at the Alamo.[26]

The hero, it would seem, is vanishing as the modern he-man finds himself carried farther and farther away from his western past by a progress-minded civilization, and the frenetic efforts of he-man magazines to retrieve heroic types from history result in hackneyed formulas and distortion. *Climax*, for example, whose very title suggests the sexually sublimated efforts of the male to establish himself and whose contents never involve heterosexual love, prints such stories as "Stranger in Town," which tells of an aging gunfighter, Tom London, who, going blind, realizes that he has not been able to keep pace with the world he once dominated. As he says, "I couldn't hunt buffalo or Indians anymore, or even white men. The only thing that's hunted anymore is animals," and the narrator informs the reader that "Tom London, the gunfighter, was a bitter man. Very bitter." And upon hearing that London is in town, the resident old-timer tells a boy, "You don't see many of his breed anymore."[27] The significance of the mythical gunfighter—one of the most enduring figures in American western lore—lies in the cultural tension it reveals. Cawelti has noted that

> both the tendency to admire gunfighter heroes and the actual social incidence of violence with guns are both symptoms of a more complex cultural force: the sense of decaying masculine potency which has long afflicted American culture....Yet, at the same time, the American tradition has always emphasized individual masculine force; Americans love to think of themselves as pioneers, men who have conquered a continent and sired on it a new society. This radical discrepancy between the sense of eroding masculinity and the view of America as a great history of men against the wilderness has created the need for a means of symbolic expression of masculine potency in an unmistakable way. This means is the gun, particularly the six-gun.[28]

The gunfighter, then, is the paradigm of the bewildered, angry male, and his gun—rife with phallic implications—has been transformed by its owner into an instrument of destruction.

Even more telling in this regard is "Tarzan of the Tetons"— i.e., the wilderness has become a jungle—in which Earl Durand finds he no longer cares to distinguish between the frontier past he loves and the present he finds droll by comparison. As a child, Durand "like boys everywhere...liked to play cowboys and Indians and stage mock gun fights between the 'bad' guys and 'good' guys" and "once Earl staged a gun battle with live .22 ammunition. His favorite role was Jesse James."[29] But Durand retained his boyhood experiences and hero worship until "at some intangible point, he had come to believe in his world of fantasy. More and more, he withdrew from the real world into himself. By day, he would roam through the forests and hills, rifle in hand, with the jubilation of an early frontiersman....He grew to distrust and hate all the institutions and symbols of civilization that were constantly reminding him that the never-never land he had created was a self-deceit."[30]

Durand's problem is not just a personal one, however, because he must still exist in the twentieth century regardless of where his mind takes him and so he, the loner, eventually collides with civilization because "during his excursions in the forest, Earl got his food like any true pioneer, by shooting wild game. It was all right as long as he stuck to birds and rabbits. But when he began to shoot deer and elk indiscriminately, in and out of season, he ran into trouble with the law."[31] Now, in 1939, the natural impulses of the pioneer must be suppressed and ordered by the laws of civilized men and Durand, unable to accept this restriction, flees from his fantasy, triggering in him a desire for the last stand made famous by his mythological heroes. Thus, he robs a bank surrounded by vigilantes and is shot to death. As the narrator tells us, "the truth is that Earl wasn't interested in money. This was the climax of a warped dream—Jesse James at his most glorious. For a fleeting moment, the street resembled the wild past of Dodge City."[32] There is another truth to be considered, though, because Earl Durand remains the sympathetic hero throughout the story and if, as we are told, his dream is warped, it is only because he, unlike the he-men who read about him, attempted to live his frontier past realistically rather than ritualistically.

Realizing the folly of Earl Durand's methods, the he-man attempts to gain a similar rapport with the past while conducting his activities within the limitations placed on him by the present. In the words of Sigmund Freud, he "shows an intention of making [him]self independent of the external by seeking satisfaction in internal pyschical processes...satisfaction is obtained from illusions, which are recognized as such without the discrepancy between them and reality being allowed to interfere with enjoyment."[33] Durand at his happiest is a Natty Bumppo figure who finds peace in a harmonious relationship with nature, yet in doing so he appears insane to his contemporaries who likewise feel an urge toward primitivism and become predators who enforce society's laws by tracking Durand to his death. They do this while admiring, even perhaps envying, him for his willingness to reject the civilization they both represent and despise. Once again, Freud defines the phenomenon when he says that

> we cannot see why the regulations made by ourselves should not...be a protection and a benefit for every one of us. And yet, when we consider how unsuccessful we have been in precisely this field of prevention of suffering, a suspicion dawns on us that here, too, a piece of unconquerable nature may lie behind—this time a piece of our own psychical constitution. When we start considering this possibility, we come upon a contention which is so astonishing that we must dwell upon it. This contention holds that what we call our civilization is largely responsible for our misery, and that we should be much happier if we gave it up and returned to primitive conditions.[34]

This return is impossible for the modern he-man in any literal sense—as it probably is for all members of civilized society—but he can act out and thereby express his urge to achieve it. Or he can read about it in he-man magazines and gain a vicarious satisfaction in doing so. Either way, the emphasis must always be on the individual, since to escape or to reject society's collective restraints requires a solitary act or state of mind. The "rugged individual," often thought of in an industrial context but certainly not limited to it by any definition, is one who does the extraordinary thing and does it alone. The he-man, an advocate of rugged individualism, acts and thinks accordingly. It would, of course, be simpler (and less costly) to buy meat in the modern supermarket but that in itself says little about a person that could not be said of countless others. Slotkin has found that "the hunter myth sanctifies the activities of a Crockett as ends in themselves, independent of their function as part of the progressive extension of civilization and progress.... Such a hunter is not concerned with producing carcasses of beasts for the use of the population, whether for food or clothing. The sole uses of the creatures are as occasions for the exercise of his hunting passion and prowess, for it is this exercise that proves him a man."[35] It is the way of the mountain man, the cowboy, the frontiersman of whatever stripe who is, for the modern American, a quasi-primitive predator surviving in a hostile land. Thus, the he-man gains—vicariously through action or reading—a sense of freedom and self-reliance he can find in no other way. Freud's study of the individual in a mass society confirms this view of the he-man:

> The liberty of the individual is no gift of civilization. It was greater before there was any civilization, though then, it is true, it had for the most part no value, since the individual was scarcely in a position to defend it. The development of civilization imposes restrictions on it, and justice demands that no one shall escape those restrictions.... A good part of the struggles of mankind centre round the single task of finding an expedient accommodation—one, that is, that will bring happiness—between this claim of the individual and the cultural claims of the group.[36]

Freud's "expedient accommodation" is for the he-man his very he-manliness, an overpowering sense of masculinity pitted against society's efforts to reduce it to manageable proportions. With an inarticulate awareness of the masculine tradition he has inherited from the Age of Jackson through the Gilded Age to the present—a mesh of anti-female, anti-intellectual anxieties— the he-man sees himself as a rebel, even an endangered species, who seeks refuge in a nineteenth-century perspective and gains encouragement from his magazines. Thus, *Argosy* carries such articles as "The Vigilantes Are Back!" which declares that "breaking the law out West is a dangerous business these days. The Vigilantes are back riding the range and they mean business!"[37] These men are not a legally established law enforcement group but individuals who come together just long enough to enforce the law as they understand it. An Idaho vigilante is quoted as saying "We're filled with the true spirit of the Old West. Our main mission is protecting ranch land and property. Our targets are rustlers, vandals, environmentalists, hippies, state fish and game people, hunters and anybody else who forgets who owns the land."[38] Relying on a laissez-faire point of view traceable to Jacksonian thought and a might-makes-right mentality whose heyday was the Gilded Age, the he-man is incapable of possessing the double vision that would enable him to see contradictions. With his single-minded devotion to his own preservation, he finds nothing amiss in hunters hunting hunters, law and order used as the basis for fighting those whose job it is to enforce law and order ("fish and game people"), protecting the land by chasing away environmentalists, or espousing the supremacy of the individual by marking individualists ("hippies") for persecution. To the vigilante he-man, these people are as faceless as the Indian, the Oriental, and the European immigrants were to his forefathers in the last century.

In the same issue of *Argosy*, an article praises film star Charles Bronson who, billed as a "man of action," made a movie in 1974 depicting a one-man vigilante effort to clean up America. The movie was called *Death Wish*. In *Stag*, "The Secret Mission of Marcus Whitman" provides still another he-man hero who fought his way through blizzards and Indians to convince the president that the Oregon Territory should be owned by the United States. As the story states, "there must have been a touch of madness about the buckskin-suited doctor. For no one in his right mind would have tried to do what he did—not even to save Oregon."[39] But of course he did do it and thereby achieved an important accommodation by working for the inevitable civilizing process yet doing so in a rugged, individualistic way. Nature has been defeated by Whitman, and he can return to family and community, his manliness affirmed by the severity of the test and his nomination for a place in he-man history secured.

Yet while ventures into the wilderness and mock primitivism may offer a sense of freedom and more excitement than the supermarket, not all American he-men are reincarnated frontiersmen with a rifle, and the rite of passage can assume forms other than the hunting trip and feigned survival against nature. The difference lies in how boy he-men are raised, and they will first prove, then reaffirm, their manliness accordingly. Rugged individualism continues to influence whatever manly means are chosen because it is the dominant hope for relief from civilization's constraints and conformity. Anxiety, a primary emotion, results from these and has become so pervasive that relief in life must be found in brushes with death itself, either through a variety of bizarre activities or by observing violence among others. The wilderness, after all, is vanishing, and what remains is overrun with rugged individuals to the point that the term and the concepts it represents are in danger of being eradicated by the men who believe in them: the culmination of Daniel Boone's fear that someday he might not be able to chop down a tree so that its top would land at the door of his cabin.[40] This means different ways of asserting manliness, discovering a sense of freedom, and stressing individuality must be found: new frontiers of courage, strength, and endurance in which death is an ever-present possibility.

He-man magazines document this phenomenon in the stories and articles they print. "The Flying Fool" tells of a "legendary lone-wolf dogfighter who took on 100 German planes"[41] while in the same issue of *Stag* "238,857 Miles of Sex" promises to reveal an incomparable test of endurance that not only recalls nineteenth-century male attitudes toward women as objects to be conquered but also magnifies to an absurdity Leslie Fiedler's thesis that love and death are inextricably linked in the American mind. Titles from other magazines are equally revealing: "Defying Death and Taming Fear at the Circus"(*Argosy*, April 1975); "Man-Eating Quartet of Luawata" (*Saga*, December 1974); "America's Merry Slit-Your-Throat Soldiers" (*Climax*, December 1961); "Ski-Hunt for Sharks"(*True*, September 1966); "The Transatlantic Balloon Hustler Has a 50-50 Chance of Surviving" (*True*, December 1974); and "He Flies...He Floats...He Flirts with Death" (*True*, November 1966). It appears inescapable that in he-man literature, the ultimate risk is accepted as a means of proving manliness.

This proof requires action not only in the negative sense of alleviating anxiety but in the positive sense of asserting he-man superiority over the world he inhabits. And that world, when it is not mundane, is rife with anxiety caused by the two major roles assigned him: family man and working man. A biographical article in *True*, "Bless You, Damn You...Love, Dad: The Confessions of an American Father," lays open the trauma of the modern he-man:

> No amount of planning or lectures could synchronize car-sickness accidents or impromptu pee-pee stops. No, 20 minutes after one had swabbed, scoured, and sprayed against Shirley's bodily rejects, Ronnie or Leah demanded equal time and attention. Young kidneys refused to function at gas stops and then, three miles later, in open if impossibly public country, couldn't contain themselves. One dread day featured a dozen kiddie distress stops, a blown tire, a costly speeding ticket, roadside disciplines and a climactic mommy-daddy quarrel; I gained little more ground that day than had the early prairie schooners.[42]

Beyond the obvious tension conveyed in this passage, it is interesting on three counts. First, the family scene is described primarily in excremental terms, and the tone is one of revulsion ("swabbed, scoured, and sprayed") as well as irritation. Second, the author views the whole ordeal and the trip itself not as a shared experience but as a conspiracy against his personal sanity and progress. He thus concludes that "I gained little ground ...that day" as though the trip held no significance for anyone but himself. Finally, the passage ends with an analogy between the author's own tedious life and frontier life. While this may seem to contradict the notion that the he-man yearns to recapture his nineteenth-century past, in fact it corroborates it because, for better or for worse, he uses that past as a reference point of stability for his own identity. Then, shortly thereafter, the article defines the other tension-filled world inhabited by the male:

> It's tougher at the bottom. Or, more especially, in that great American middle where cultural, religious, social and economic

devils dare one to remove one's nose from the grindstone for a
moment. One works unceasingly to keep up with the Joneses,
who somehow appear to outrace him at every turn. . . . When
daddy seeks relief in extra-marital sex, he is at once spending
money badly needed at home and threatening the only security
available to his child-burdened wife.[43]

These lines are important not just for what they say about the
working man's psychosexual anxiety but for their candid men-
tioning of illicit sex as a way, however futile, to gain temporary
relief. This kind of sex is finally unsatisfactory because relief
from one set of anxieties is hardly to be found in still another,
namely, guilt. Thus, the male finds himself both tied to a woman
and in need of a woman he cannot have (again, one thinks of
George Babbitt), each situation posing a female threat to his
masculinity. The result is, at best, a distrust of women beyond
their ability to provide sexual gratification; at worst, it is misog-
yny in one form or another.

Examples of the masculinity cult's attitudes toward women
abound in he-man literature. In *Climax*, "Booze and Babes at
Canaveral" tells how liquor and sex can be used in equal doses
to relieve the tensions of the space race, the technological *coup
de grace* against nature by progress-oriented males who believe
in social Darwinism even though they have never heard of it or
of Herbert Spencer: "Bottles of booze and lots of babes; soft
lights and sweet music—sometimes wild and swinging. That's
the off-duty pattern for our hardworking rocketmen, the guys
who dicker with the future."[44] In another article, "The French
Take It with Them," women serve men sexually to help them
forget the horrors of war: "France's fierce jungle fighters didn't
have to wait for a leave or a weekend pass to see a girl—they
had 'em right with them at the front!"[45]

Taking a different tack, "White Slave of Melville Island" (a
crudely pirated version of Herman Melville's *Typee*) demon-
strates the female threat to masculinity in two ways. Horace
Phillips, an American sailor stranded on a South Pacific island,
tells of being captured by aborigines and forced to remove all
his clothing. His initial embarrassment, however, soon shifts to

dismay because the native women take scant notice of his exposed phallus. Then, as if that were not enough, he is made a slave to a woman and compelled to do her work—washing, cooking, and carrying water. He escapes, of course, and delivers his account in *Stag*, calling the experience a "nightmare."[46]

Finally, *True* magazine has given fuller expression to the promale, anti-female mentality outlined in its subscription advertisement cited earlier. In an essay titled "The Big Squeal," the he-man is seen digging in his heels against the rush of modern trends, his strength derived from a mixture of disgust for and fear of women. The threat is nothing less than imminent symbolic castration unless it can be countered in the way suggested by the picture accompanying the essay: a shot from the movie *Public Enemy* shows James Cagney smashing half a grapefruit into his wife's face. Ironically, the he-man, often a tough law-and-order figure, takes for his model a crook who defies society, the implication being that when male superiority is threatened, nothing—including country—is too dear. The character Cagney portrays is, after all, a businessman of sorts whose passions are directed toward limitless profit by whatever means necessary, and restraining women and stifling domesticity must be stopped without hesitation. Early in the essay, therefore, feigned self-criticism is used to underscore the potential dangers of women in general and marriage in particular: "Yet men are undoubtedly the worst choosers of women that God could create. Probably it's that men don't expect a hell of a lot from them in the first place, and so they go ganging into the whole thing without checking to see whether all the nuts and bolts are there. But, brother, once that sale's made, there simply ain't no refund on the purchase. It's not 10 to 20—it's life. One way or another."[47] Here, in a flurry of mixed metaphors, women are machines bought by men, and a wrong choice leads to prison, meaning, one assumes, that freedom lies in the right—or super-masculine—choice. Picking up the wilderness theme, this male manifesto continues:

> A man is a natural pursuer. The only substantial monogamists in the animal world are coyotes and wolves, and you'll notice they're not too damn particular about their diets. Women used

to accept this proclivity of man, if they were really women and
confident about it. Women are natural killers. If physical abilities
were commensurate, they would be better hunters....But somehow the gun is the primary extension of the man and somehow
the woman knows this. A good gun to a man is a companion,
an absolute, in which everything works and nothing talks back.
A man understands this. Needs it. But the Wild Bunch [feminists]
haven't gotten this together yet. They're still scratching their poi-
son oak.[48]

Hunting expresses masculinity, the rifle being a symbolic phallus and, it follows, the shot providing a climactic moment when
nature—a traditionally female figure—succumbs to an overpowering force. And given the he-man's intense affection for
his gun to the extent that he personifies it as a companion, it is
of at least passing interest to compare the passage cited above
with a portion of the Marine Corps Rifleman's Creed: "My rifle
is my best friend. It is my life. I must master it as I master my
life....My rifle is human, even as I, because it is my life. Thus,
I will learn it as a brother....We will become part of each other."[49]
The he-man hunter and the he-man soldier are one in their
obsessive, masculine identification with guns and their aggressive maintenance of superiority. Both define themselves by their
ability to subdue, whether it be man against nature or man
against other, weaker (i.e., effeminate), men. This, in turn, explains why he-man magazines print roughly equal numbers of
western and war stories, the he-man may be dressed in either
hunter's clothing or a military uniform, and there is no sub-
stantial difference between the long-distance killing of an animal
and the bomber pilot mentality. Similarly, the male's fear of
civilization's efforts to reduce him to the merely human along
with women, children, and lesser males (or, in the case of the
military he-man, civilians) is expressed in "The Big Squeal" when
the author declares that the "Gloria Whosits and whoever started
the current thrombosis are city women. Cities, particularly the
suburban occlusions, are run by women."[50] The city represents
civilization, confinement, and female efforts to domesticate the
world. The threatened male, therefore, periodically flees to the
wilderness either of nature or war to discover his maleness in

nihilistic experience, to regain the predatory life of the frontier or the battleground and thereby regain himself.

Like Buffalo Bill Cody, the modern he-man is caught between two worlds, so much so, in fact, that he takes various parts of one world with him when he leaves it to enter the other. He can shed neither one completely nor would he want to because each world satisfies certain needs—motherly comfort and order plus material wealth on one side, rugged individualism on the other. Thus, he takes his technology with him in the form of machines when he travels to the wilderness and then returns to civilization a better man for having roughed it, evidenced by the dirt, the weariness, and the dead animals which accompany him home.

Concerning the machine in particular, the masculinity cult has adopted it as an integral part of the he-man personality and lifestyle. The machine is, in concept at least, imposing in its power, strength, noise, and endurance under rugged conditions. Yet even here distinctions must be drawn because, in actuality, not all machines suggest the same qualities. The refrigerator, for instance, is passive and domestic while the automobile, often considered a masculine machine, may or may not supply masculine identification. The man who reads *Playboy* uses the car but not so much for what it does as for what it says about the owner in terms of social status, wealth, and subtle sexuality. The he-man, however, is concerned with action rather than implication so that in all probability he was an adolescent hot-rodder who, in adulthood, still drives an overpowered, large car rather than a smaller, sophisticated one. Yet the automobile remains a secondary machine for the he-man because it is limited for the most part to domestic and job-related transportation. In other words, it, too, is limited in what it can do, and the he-man, living as he does in a world that had made the frontiersman's horse impractical and obsolete, must find a satisfactory substitute.

He can and often does use a four-wheel-drive vehicle or other type of mechanized pack mule for his treks into the wilderness, but his literature indicates that two other kinds of machines serve masculine ends above all others: the snowmobile and the motorcyle, especially the latter. The machine is in the garden and, according to an article in *True*, "in a car, you're always in a compartment and everything you see is just more TV. . . . On a cycle you're completely in contact with it all. You're in the scene, not just watching it, and the sense of presence is overwhelming."[51] Here, the machine is not only in the garden, it is an organic part of the garden. This idyllic rapport between man, motorcycle, and landscape is not typical, though. Rather, this particular machine (the snowmobile is little more than a winterized motorcycle) is most often utilized by he-men to accomplish the opposite effect since aggression rather than harmony, assertion rather than acceptance, defines masculinity. Similar to the gun in hunting, the motorcycle possesses a sexuality to be used as an assertion of virility and male dominance over female nature: like the horse, the motorcycle is mounted and controlled with the arms and hands, the powerful engine between the legs under the total control of the rider. In this fashion, the he-man assaults the landscape, bludgeoning it as he goes and merging in the process the modern man and his frontier mentality via his sexual, mechanical horse which is noisier, more rugged, than the animal. Or, as an article called "Motocross: Hills, Dales, Bumps and Mud" states, "the start of a motocross race is a combination of Times Square at rush hour and the corraling of a herd of cattle into a branding pen."[52]

He-men need machines to help them retain and assert he-manliness, and they bear the same obsessive affection for them that they feel for the guns that are used for similar, predatory reasons. According to a French observer, the American loves his machines "as a lover loves his mistress."[53] Moreover, the machine proves handy as a rite of passage devised by men who require violence with its ever-present threat of death. This would explain "Polo with 4-Wheel Ponies" and the sport it describes: "Autoball is a simple, rough game: a brave man called a referee throws a ball to the center of the field and then runs for his life as the autos zoom in at top speed with players leaning perilously out to make the first scoop."[54] These men—cowboys in cars— are not emulating the refined, aristocratic sport of polo but reducing it to their he-manly level, thereby voicing their western predecessor's disdain for the stereotyped eastern esthete who pursues effeminate ideals and interests rather than masculine ones. "The Big Squeal," for example, describes a male dancer as "some ballet job who couldn't leave a footprint if he walked over your kid's sandpile."[55]

The he-man, it seems, accepts such qualities of life as brutality, pathological hatred and its opposite, self-assertion, though not always consciously, perhaps, but in terms of unconscious traditions and historical motivations as revealed through his actions, attitudes, and lifestyle. While many, including environmentalists, cry out against a technological devastation of art, nature, and the values they embody, the he-man mounts his machine, loads his gun, and proceeds to assault both: art as passive sissiness, nature as proving ground. This is what his forefathers did in and to the frontier to assert their superior strength and fortitude, and they alone are worthy of hero status. Necessity becomes ritual, and masculine activities become a device for countering the female domination of home and city and for bringing "the American man and American values back from the shadows. . . . Back from behind the frivolous skirts of libbers."[56] The alternative is unrelieved anxiety, the bathos of equality, and the he-man ethic—kept alive through generations of sons from Andrew Jackson to the present—works with all the masculinity it can muster to avoid it.

NOTES

INTRODUCTION

heavily graded reading

1. Geoffrey Gorer, *The American People*, rev. ed. (New York: W. W. Norton, 1964), pp. 23-49.

2. Ibid., p. 53.

3. James Fenimore Cooper, *Notions of the Americans*, II (Philadelphia: n.p., 1836), pp. 227-28.

4. John Demos, "The American Family in Past Time," *The American Scholar*, 43 (Summer 1974), 436.

5. John Higham, "From Boundlessnesss to Consolidation," William L. Clements Library, 1969; rpt. in *The Bobbs-Merrill Reprint Series in American History*, No. H-414, pp. 11, 15.

6. Elizabeth Fox-Genovese, "Psychohistory versus Psychodeterminism," *Reviews in American History*, 3 (December 1975), 414.

7. See Erik H. Erikson, *Childhood and Society*, 2d ed. (New York: W. W. Norton, 1963), pp. 283-84.

8. Bertram Wyatt-Brown, "The Abolitionist Controversy," in *Men, Women, and Issues in American History*, ed. Howard H. Quint and Milton Cantor (Homewood, Ill.: Dorsey Press, 1975), I, 216.

CHAPTER 1. THE JACKSONIAN MYSTIQUE

1. Marvin Meyers, *The Jacksonian Persuasion*, 2d ed. (Stanford, Calif.: Stanford Univ. Press, 1960), p. 10.

2. John Higham, "From Boundlessness to Consolidation," William L. Clements Library, 1969; rpt. in *The Bobbs-Merrill Reprint Series in American History*, No. H-414, p. 6.

3. Ibid., p. 6.

4. Ibid., p. 10.

5. Ibid., p. 11.

6. Bertram Wyatt-Brown, "The Abolitionist Controversy," in *Men, Women, and Issues in American History*, ed. Howard H. Quint and Milton Cantor (Homewood, Ill.: Dorsey Press, 1975), I, 216.

7. Higham, "From Boundlessness to Consolidation," p. 13.

8. Geoffrey Gorer, *The American People*, rev. ed. (New York: W. W. Norton, 1964), pp. 29-30.

9. Ibid., p. 30.

10. Ibid., p. 56.

11. Ibid., pp. 56-57.

12. Leslie A. Fiedler, *Love and Death in the American Novel*, 2d ed. (New York: Stein and Day, 1966), p. 26.

13. Philip Young, "Fallen from Time," in *Psychoanalysis and American Fiction*, ed. Irving Malin (New York: E. P. Dutton, 1965), p. 42.

14. Washington Irving, "Rip Van Winkle," in *Washington Irving*, ed. Stanley T. Williams (New York: Holt, Rinehart and Winston, 1950), p. 94. Subsequent references are to this edition; page numbers will be provided in the text.

15. Young, "Fallen from Time," p. 44.

16. Fiedler, *Love and Death*, p. 26.

17. Ibid., p. 27.

18. Meyers, *Jacksonian Persuasion*, pp. 50-51.

19. Ibid., p. 14.

20. Ibid., pp. 17-18.

21. James D. Richardson, ed., *Messages and Papers of the Presidents, 1789-1897* (Washington, D.C.: n.p., 1896), III, 305.

22. Richard Hofstadter, *Anti-Intellectualism in American Life* (New York: Vintage, 1962), p. 154. The fear of high culture was Enlightenment doctrine and formed one of the bases for the Revolution. Distrust of the upper class was not, therefore, a purely Jacksonian phenomenon, though it exploded in heated, often irrational, rhetoric to become an internal political issue during the first decades of the last century.

23. James Fenimore Cooper, *Notions of the Americans* (Philadelphia: n.p., 1836), II, 227-28.

24. James Fenimore Cooper, *Home as Found* (1838; rpt. New York: Capricorn, 1961), p. 285.

25. Cited in John William Ward, *Andrew Jackson* (New York: Oxford Univ. Press, 1962), p. 2.

26. Richard Slotkin, *Regeneration through Violence* (Middletown, Conn.: Wesleyan Univ. Press, 1973), p. 397.

27. Henry Nash Smith, *Virgin Land* (Cambridge: Harvard Univ. Press, 1950), pp. 54-55.

28. Ibid., p. 55.

29. Slotkin, *Regeneration through Violence*, p. 410.

30. Ibid., p. 411; John A. McClung, *Sketches of Western Adventure* (Maysville, Ky.: n.p., 1832), pp. 45, 49, and 86. As Slotkin points out, McClung's book enjoyed broad circulation since it went through nine editions between 1832 and 1839, several of them being issued from such important publishing centers as Philadelphia and Cincinnati.

31. Ward, *Andrew Jackson*, pp. 46-78. The term is the title of a chapter dealing with the Jackson-Adams confrontation.

32. Ibid., pp. 76-77.

33. Cited in Hofstadter, *Anti-Intellectualism*, p. 159.

34. Ibid., p. 162.

35. Slotkin, *Regeneration through Violence*, p. 411.

36. Ibid., p. 412.

37. Smith, *Virgin Land*, p. 81.

38. Slotkin, *Regeneration through Violence*, p. 413.

39. Ibid.; William H. Goetzmann, "The Mountain Man as Jacksonian Man," in *The American Culture*, ed. Hennig Cohen (Boston: Houghton Mifflin, 1968), pp. 68-70.

40. Cited in Ward, *Andrew Jackson*, p. 25.

41. Ibid.

42. Samuel Putnam Waldo, *Memoirs of Andrew Jackson*, 3d ed. (Hartford, Conn.: n.p., 1819), p. 12.

43. Nathaniel H. Claiborne, *Notes on the War in the South* (Richmond, Va.: n.p., 1819), p. 69.

44. D. H. Lawrence, *Studies in Classical American Literature* (1923; rpt. New York: Viking, 1964), p. 50.

45. Richardson, *Messages and Papers of the Presidents*, III, 305.

46. Meyers, *Jacksonian Persuasion*, p. 32.

47. Ibid., p. 44.

48. Alexis de Tocqueville, *Democracy in America*, trans. Henry Reeves (1850; rpt. New York: A. S. Barnes, 1858), II, 144-45.

49. Edward Pessen, *Jacksonian America* (Homewood, Ill.: Dorsey Press, 1969), p. 40.

50. Tocqueville, *Democracy in America*, II, 146.

51. See Gorer, *American People*, p. 60.

52. The phrase "male-oriented culture" is not intended to suggest that America was or is unique in this regard. All major western cultures have been male-oriented, most of them more so than American culture. Rather, it is the peculiarly American variation on this theme made possible by a unique set of circumstances that is the object of this investigation. It can, moreover, be argued that while America may be male-oriented, it is female-dominated, given the concept of the female super-ego in the national consciousness. American males do try periodically to shed this consciousness, but it remains pervasive nonetheless. Whatever, a powerful sense of masculinity in America is not unique but uniquely American: e.g., in many other societies, masculinity is expressed in aggressive sexuality; in America, masculinity often involves displaced, or sublimated, sexuality.

53. Erik H. Erikson, *Childhood and Society*, 2d ed. (New York: W. W. Norton, 1963), p. 287.

54. Cited in Pessen, *Jacksonian America*, p. 177.

55. Wyatt-Brown, "Abolitionist Controversy," p. 216.

56. Ibid., p. 219.

57. Ibid., p. 222.

58. Ibid., p. 223.

59. Ibid., pp. 223-24.

60. Ibid., p. 224.

61. Ibid., p. 233.

62. Ibid.

63. Samuel A. Cartwright, "Eulogy Delivered at Natchez, Miss., July 12, 1845," Dusenbery, comp., *Monument*, p. 302; cited in Ward, *Andrew Jackson*, p. 44.

64. *Richmond Enquirer*, 3 January 1828; *The New York Times*, 8 October 1834; see also Ward, *Andrew Jackson*, pp. 51, 53.

65. O. L. Holley, *The Connexion between the Mechanic Arts and the Welfare of the States* (Troy, N.Y.: n.p., 1825), p. 4; cited in Ward, *Andrew Jackson*, p. 170.

66. Ward, *Andrew Jackson*, pp. 168-69; see also David Riesman, et al., *The Lonely Crowd* (New Haven, Conn.: Yale University Press, 1950), pp. 14-15. Riesman does, I think, give too much credit to nineteenth-century men as inner-directed since much of the concept of rugged individualism was mythical, and men as often as not moved with the crowd in spirit if not in fact. That they believed in individualism in the abstract cannot, however, be denied.

67. Cited in Richard Hofstadter, *The American Political Tradition and the Men Who Made It* (New York: Vintage, 1948), p. 57.

68. Ibid., p. 62.

69. Michael Paul Rogin, *Fathers and Children* (New York: Alfred A. Knopf, 1975), pp. 254-55, 288. Rogin's study of what he sees as Jackson's obsession with the Indian question is uneven. On the one hand, for example, he provides perceptive, psychoanalytical analyses of the language of Jackson and Jacksonians concerning Indians. On the other hand, however, he concludes too much from what he claims was Jackson's child rage without relating enough about Jackson's early, splintered family life. Elsewhere, he states that "the conquest of the Indian made the country uniquely American" (p. 7), a dubious generalization unless one is also willing to believe that the British conquest of natives, or the French or Spanish, made those nations unique, too. Rather, America's uniqueness required a combination of factors, not one act of genocide carried out over two-and-a-half centuries. The use of Rogin's work here will, therefore, be tempered by an effort to distill his best insights from his questionable ones. For a thoughtfully critical review of *Fathers and Children*, see Elizabeth Fox-Genovese's "Psychohistory versus Psychodeterminism," *Reviews in American History*, 3 (December 1975), 407-18.

70. Jackson to Thomas Cadwalader, 16 November 1828, in John Spencer Bassett, ed., *Correspondence of Andrew Jackson* (Washington, D.C.: n.p., 1928), III, 445; cited in Rogin, *Fathers and Children*, p. 284.

71. Rogin, *Fathers and Children*, pp. 288-89; Frederick Robinson, "A Program for Labor," in Joseph L. Blau, ed., *Social Theories of Jacksonian Democracy* (New York: Liberal Arts Press, 1947), p. 338.

72. Richardson, *Messages and Papers of the Presidents*, III, 554-55; see also Meyers, *Jacksonian Persuasion*, p. 161 and Rogin, *Fathers and Children*, pp. 290-91.

73. Hofstadter, *American Political Tradition*, p. 67.

74. Erikson, *Childhood and Society*, pp. 304-5.

75. W. W. Rostow, *The Stages of Economic Growth* (Cambridge: Harvard Univ. Press, 1960), p. 7.

76. Leo Marx, *The Machine in the Garden* (New York: Oxford Univ. Press, 1964), p. 27.

77. Ibid.

78. Ibid., p. 69.

79. Ibid., p. 29.

80. Gorer, *American People*, p. 53.

81. John Bunyan, *The Pilgrim's Progress* (1677; rpt. New York: James Pott and Co., n.d.), pp. 4-5.

82. Marx, *Machine in the Garden*, p. 208.

83. Herman Melville, *Moby-Dick*, ed. Harrison Hayford and Hershel Parker (1851; rpt. New York: W. W. Norton, 1967), p. 147.

84. Ward, *Andrew Jackson*, p. 193.

85. Henry David Thoreau, *Walden and Civil Disobedience*, ed. Owen Thomas (1854; rpt. New York: W. W. Norton, 1966), p. 5.

86. Ward, *Andrew Jackson*, p. 213.

87. Fox-Genovese, "Psychohistory versus Psychodeterminism," p. 411. The author is responding here to Rogin's mistaken attempt to separate Jackson's motives (psychological) from the common man's (economic).

CHAPTER 2. THE FEMALE FOIL

1. Alexis de Tocqueville, "Fortnight in the Wilderness," in George Wilson Pierson, *Tocqueville and Beaumont in America* (New York: Oxford Univ. Press, 1938), pp. 234-35, 239.

2. Ibid., pp. 243-44.

3. Ibid., p. 245.

4. Ibid., p. 237.

5. G. J. Barker-Benfield, *The Horrors of the Half-Known Life* (New York: Harper and Row, 1976), pp. 6-7. Barker-Benfield's study of nineteenth-century male attitudes toward women and sexuality has only a limited value, one of information rather than analysis, since the book is freighted with sensational claims cast in purple prose. As one reviewer has said of *Horrors*, "there are some worthwhile nuggets to be mined here.... The pity is that our guide resolutely holds the lantern so as to block the light." Martin Duberman, review of *The Horrors of the Half-Known Life*, *The New York Times Book Review*, 18 January 1976, pp. 4 and 15.

6. Leslie Fiedler, *Love and Death in the American Novel*, 2d ed. (New York: Stein and Day, 1966), p. 31.

7. George Rogers Taylor, *The Transportation Revolution* (New York: Harper and Row, 1968), p. vii.

8. Elizabeth F. Baker, *Technology and Woman's Work* (New York: Columbia Univ. Press, 1964), pp. 21, 24-25, 35, 42, 52-53, and 426.

9. Alexis de Tocqueville, *Democracy in America*, trans. Henry Reeves (1850; rpt. New York: A. S. Barnes, 1858), II, 218.

10. Ibid., p. 219.

11. Ibid., pp. 212-13.

12. Janice Law Trecker, "Sex, Science and Education," *American Quarterly*, 26 (October 1974), 363-64.

13. Tocqueville, *Democracy*, II, 221.

14. Ibid.

15. Ibid., pp. 221-22.

16. Barbara Welter, "The Cult of True Womanhood," *American Quarterly*, 18 (Summer 1966), 151-52.

17. Tocqueville, *Democracy*, II, 226.

18. Kathryn Kish Sklar, *Catharine Beecher* (New Haven, Conn.: Yale Univ. Press, 1973), p. xiii.

19. Ibid., p. xiv.

20. Catharine Beecher, *The Elements of Mental and Moral Philosophy, Founded upon Experience, Reason and the Bible* (Hartford, Conn.: n.p., 1831), p. 57; see also Sklar, *Catharine Beecher*, pp. 84-89.

21. Sklar, *Catharine Beecher*, pp. 85-86.

22. Beecher, *Elements*, p. 263.

23. Nathaniel Hawthorne, *The Blithedale Romance* (1852; rpt. New York: W. W. Norton, 1958), p. 137. Subsequent references are to this edition; page numbers will be provided in the text.

24. Nathaniel Hawthorne, *The Scarlet Letter*, ed. Sculley Bradley, Richmond Croom Beatty, and E. Hudson Long (1850; rpt. New York: W. W. Norton, 1961), p. 186.

25. Sklar, *Catharine Beecher*, p. 87.

26. Ibid., p. 96; Catharine Beecher, *Suggestions Respecting Improvements in Education, Presented to the Trustees* (Hartford, Conn.: Packard and Butler, 1829), p. 46, and *An Essay on the Education of Female Teachers* (New York: Van Nostrand and Dwight, 1835), p. 18.

27. Tocqueville, *Democracy*, I, 325.

28. In *Love and Death in the American Novel*, Fiedler uses the term "homoerotic" rather than "homosexual" whenever possible since the latter, he feels, is a more disturbing word (p. 349). Yet "homoerotic" poses problems, too, and so I have used "latent homosexual" in the hope that such a qualification will make clear an important distinction.

29. D. H. Lawrence's poem "Snake" is a good example of this situation. With the voice of his education telling him to be a man and to kill the serpent before him, the man in the poem is a specific example of a mytho-psychological phenomenon in western culture. America is a massive example of that same phenomenon. Likewise, after he lashes out at the snake and tries to destroy it, the man feels guilty just as America has felt a collective guilt after the fact for its treatment of nature and the Indian who was a part of it. There is, however, no going back and we are—for better or for worse—a "civilized" and progress-oriented people.

30. Fiedler, *Love and Death*, p. 355.

31. Wright Morris, "Afterword," in Richard Henry Dana, *Two Years before the Mast* (1840; rpt. New York: Signet, 1964), p. 383.

32. R.W.B. Lewis, *The American Adam* (Chicago: Univ. of Chicago Press, 1955), p. 41.

33. Gerda Lerner, "The Lady and the Mill Girl," *Mid-Continent American Studies Journal*, 10 (Spring 1969), 8.

34. Elizabeth Blackwell, forbidden to practice medicine in New York City hospitals during the 1850s, opened a medical school for women in 1868. As the first female member of the AMA, she survived efforts to oust her at the annual convention of 1876. Thus, by the mid-1870s, women had begun to infiltrate the inner circles of the medical profession.

35. Augustus Kinsley Gardner, *History of the Art of Mid-wifery* (New York: Stringer and Townshend, 1852), p. 4.

36. Donald B. Meyer, *The Positive Thinkers* (Garden City, N.Y.: Doubleday, 1965), p. 56.

37. Cited in Barker-Benfield, *Horrors*, p. 85.

38. Cited in Welter, "Cult of True Womanhood," pp. 160-61.

39. Cited in Barker-Benfield, *Horrors*, p. 93. Barker-Benfield's chapter on Sims's career is worthwhile insofar as it provides information on a previously obscure historical figure (see n. 5, this chapter). Indeed, it could be argued that Sims deserves his obscurity and should be allowed to keep it, but he was considered a leading gynecologist of his time and represents, therefore, an important faction of that medical specialty, however extreme.

40. David M. Kennedy, *Birth Control in America* (New Haven, Conn.: Yale Univ. Press, 1970), pp. 54-55. Robert Latou Dickinson was an enlightened gynecologist and an advocate of women's rights. He was thus a key figure at the turn of the century when the feminist movement gained momentum.

41. Sklar, *Catharine Beecher*, p. 206.

42. Ibid., pp. 213-14.

43. Ibid., pp. 321-22 n. 22; see also Theodore Cianfrani, *A Short History of Obstetrics and Gynecology* (Springfield, Mass.: Charles C. Thomas, 1960), pp. 300, 314.

44. Carroll Smith-Rosenberg, "The Hysterical Woman," *Social Research*, 39 (Winter 1972), 656.

45. Ibid., pp. 656-57; S. Weir Mitchell, *Doctor and Patient* (Philadelphia: J. B. Lippincott, 1887), pp. 84, 92.

46. Smith-Rosenberg, "Hysterical Woman," pp. 673-74.

47. Ibid., pp. 675-76.

48. John Demos, "The American Family in Past Time," *The American Scholar*, 43 (Summer 1974), 437.

49. Fiedler, *Love and Death*, p. 194.

50. Carroll Smith-Rosenberg and Charles Rosenberg, "The Female Animal," *The Journal of American History*, 60 (September 1973), 332.

51. Paul Topinard, *Anthropology* (London: n.p., 1878), p. 311. A table

shows that English and Scotch males have a skull capacity of 1,427 grams while women of the same extraction, though superior to other women, have a skull capacity of only 1,260 grams.

52. John S. Haller and Robin M. Haller, *The Physician and Sexuality in Victorian America* (Urbana: Univ. of Illinois Press, 1974), p. 48.

53. While notions such as these regarding woman's biological fate would seem to gain corroboration later from Freud's dictum that anatomy is destiny, they had little or none of Freud's sophisticated and landmark thinking behind them. Furthermore, these notions were often applied, however innocently, by men with cultural and masculine motives. Thus, they had a personal stake in the "truths" they upheld as undeniable. Even so, they would have been on more solid ground had they been willing to entertain the male's biological destiny as well as the female's.

54. Charles D. Meigs, *Lecture on Some of the Distinctive Characteristics of the Female. Delivered before the Class of the Jefferson Medical College, January 5, 1847* (Philadelphia: n.p., 1847), p. 5; cited in Smith-Rosenberg and Rosenberg, "Female Animal," p. 335.

55. M. L. Holbrook, *Parturition without Pain* (New York: n.p., 1882), pp. 14-15; cited in Smith-Rosenberg and Rosenberg, "Female Animal," p. 335.

56. Cited in Haller and Haller, *Physician and Sexuality*, p. 60; A. L. Smith, "Higher Education of Women and Race Suicide," *Popular Science Monthly*, 66 (1905), 466-73.

57. Smith-Rosenberg and Rosenberg, "Female Animal," pp. 339 and 340-41 n. 19.

58. Ibid., pp. 341-42.

59. T. S. Clouston, *Female Education from a Medical Point of View* (Edinburgh: n.p., 1882), p. 19; Smith-Rosenberg and Rosenberg, "Female Animal," p. 342; see also Demos, "American Family," pp. 426-27.

60. Herbert Spencer, *The Study of Sociology* (New York: n.p., 1896), pp. 342-43, 346-67.

61. M. A. Hardaker, "Science and the Woman Question," *Popular Science Monthly*, 20 (1882), 578; cited in Haller and Haller, *Physician and Sexuality*, p. 66.

62. Haller and Haller, *Physician and Sexuality*, p. 66; Hardaker, "Science and the Woman Question," p. 583.

63. Sklar, *Catharine Beecher*, p. 113.

64. Sarah Josepha Hale, *Sketches of American Character* (Boston: n.p., 1838), p. 255; cited in William R. Taylor, *Cavalier and Yankee* (New York: George Braziller, 1961), p. 356 n. 42.

65. Taylor, *Cavalier and Yankee*, p. 121.

66. Sklar, *Catharine Beecher*, pp. 136-37, 156.

67. Ibid., pp. 194-95; see also Daniel Scott Smith, "Child-Naming Patterns and Family Structure Change"(Paper prepared for the Clark University Conference on the Family and Social Structure, 27-29 April 1972), p. 29, and Demos, "American Family," pp. 432-33. Demos also views the nineteenth century as a period of loss for women when contrasted to the previous century and to what men were accomplishing from the time of Jackson on: "...the nineteenth-century American woman, when compared to her grandmothers in Colonial times, had given up a great deal" (p. 433).

68. Haller and Haller, *Physician and Sexuality*, p. 68.

69. William K. Brooks, "The Condition of Women from a Zoological Point of View," *Popular Science Monthly*, 15 (1879), 149-50.

70. George F. Talbot, "The Political Rights and Duties of Women," *Popular Science Monthly*, 49 (1896), 84-85. Talbot's fear of black political power would, only a few years later, be projected in the immensely popular movie *Birth of a Nation*.

71. Carl N. Degler, *Out of Our Past*, rev. ed. (1959; rpt. New York: Harper and Row, 1970), pp. 357-58. See also Stanley M. Elkins, *Slavery*, 2d ed. (Chicago: Univ. of Chicago Press, 1968), pp. 130-33. Since the status of women was comparable not only to the black's but also to the child's, Elkins's slave-as-Sambo thesis offers additional insight into the patriarchal psychology of the WASP male.

72. Carl N. Degler, "What Ought to Be and What Was," *American Historical Review*, 79 (December 1974), 1477.

73. Ibid., p. 1490.

74. See Haller and Haller, *Physician and Sexuality*, pp. 82-85. "Nature's nuns" echoes Tocqueville's description of the home as a "cloister" for the woman (see n. 11).

75. Ibid., p. 84.

76. Trecker, "Sex, Science and Education," p. 353.

77. Kennedy, *Birth Control*, p. 63; William Acton, *The Functions and Disorders of the Reproductive Organs in Childhood, Youth, Adult Age, and Advanced Life Considered in Their Physiological, Social, and Moral Relations*, 3d Amer. ed. (Philadelphia: n.p., 1871), p. 164; cited in Haller and Haller, *Physician and Sexuality*, p. 100.

78. Demos, "American Family," p. 436. The added emphasis is mine.

79. Harold Frederic, *The Damnation of Theron Ware* (1896; rpt. New York: Holt, Rinehart and Winston, 1960), p. 223. Subsequent references are to this edition; page numbers will be provided in the text.

80. Fiedler, *Love and Death*, p. 270.

81. Ibid.

82. Samuel Langhorne Clemens (Mark Twain), *Adventures of Huckleberry Finn*, ed. Sculley Bradley, Richmond Croom Beatty, and E. Hudson Long (1885; rpt. New York: W. W. Norton, 1961), p. 226.

83. Fiedler, *Love and Death*, p. 337.

84. Ibid., pp. 338-39.

85. Eliza B. Duffey, *The Relations of the Sexes* (New York: n.p., 1876), p. 219.

86. George Santayana, *Character and Opinion in the United States* (1920; rpt. New York: Charles Scribner's Sons, 1921), pp. 178-80.

87. Cited in Ronald G. Walters, ed., *Primers for Prudery* (Englewood Cliffs, N.J.: Prentice-Hall, 1974), pp. 20-21. Graham, a clergyman and dietician, began delivering morality lectures in the 1830s. See also Sylvester Graham, *Chastity, In a Course of Lectures to Young Men; Intended also, for the Serious Consideration of Parents and Guardians* (New York: Fowler and Wells, n.d.), pp. i-ii; and Catharine E. Beecher and Harriet Beecher Stowe, *The American Woman's Home* (New York: J. B. Ford, 1869), pp. 285-86.

88. Welter, "Cult of True Womanhood," pp. 158-59.

89. Peter Gabriel Filene, *Him/Her/Self* (New York: New American Library, 1974), p. 83.

90. Ibid.

91. Ibid.

92. Ibid.

93. See Fiedler, *Love and Death*, pp. 25-31, 337-90.

94. Cited in Haller and Haller, *Physician and Sexuality*, pp. 126-27.

CHAPTER 3. THE JACKSONIAN LEGACY

1. John Higham, "From Boundlessness to Consolidation," William L. Clements Library, 1969; rpt. in *The Bobbs-Merrill Reprint Series in American History*, No. H-414, p. 19.

2. Ibid. See pp. 24-26 for a fuller discussion of the Civil War in these terms.

3. Robert H. Wiebe, *The Search for Order, 1877-1920* (New York: Hill and Wang, 1967), p. 14.

4. Ibid., p. 65.

5. Thorstein Veblen, "The Captain of Industry," in *Absentee Ownership and Businesss Enterprise in Recent Times*, 1923; rpt. in Gail Kennedy, ed., *Democracy and the Gospel of Wealth* (Boston: D. C. Heath, 1949), p. 106.

6. Ibid., p. 107.

7. *Nation*, 10 (9 June 1870), 367; cited in Nathan G. Hale, *Freud and the Americans* (New York: Oxford Univ. Press, 1971), p. 34.

8. Hale, *Freud and the Americans*, pp. 34-35.

9. J. H. Kellogg, *Plain Facts for Both Sexes* (1879; rpt. Battle Creek, Mich.: Good Health Publishing Co., 1910), pp. 259-60; cited in Hale, *Freud and the Americans*, p. 37.

10. Thomas C. Cochran and William Miller, *A Social History of Industrial America*, rev. ed. (New York: Harper and Brothers, 1961), p. 59.

11. Ibid., p. 129.

12. Ibid., p. 130.

13. Stanley Diamond, *In Search of the Primitive* (New Brunswick, N.J.: Transaction Books, 1974), pp. 10-11.

14. Richard Hofstadter, *The American Political Tradition and the Men Who Made It* (New York: Vintage, 1948), p. 164.

15. Ibid., pp. 164-65.

16. Ibid., pp. 176-77.

17. Richard Hofstadter, *Anti-Intellectualism in American Life* (New York: Vintage, 1962), p. 186.

18. Letter to *The New York Times*, 17 June 1880; cited in Hofstadter, *Anti-Intellectualism*, p. 188.

19. *Congressional Record*, 49th Congress, 1st Session (26 March 1886), p. 2786.

20. Cited in Hofstadter, *American Political Tradition*, p. 177.

21. Wiebe, *Search for Order*, p. 77.

22. Hofstadter, *American Political Tradition*, p. 177.

23. Alfred R. Conkling, *Life and Letters of Roscoe Conkling* (New York: n.p., 1889), pp. 540-41.

24. Elmira *Advertiser*, 6 October 1877, as reported in Thomas Collier Platt, *Autobiography* (New York: n.p., 1910), pp. 93-95.

25. Hofstadter, *Anti-Intellectualism*, p. 190.

26. William Wasserstrom, *Heiress of All the Ages* (Minneapolis: Univ. of Minnesota Press, 1959), p. vii.

27. Peter Gabriel Filene, *Him/Her/Self* (New York: New American Library, 1974), p. 83.

28. Thorstein Veblen, *The Theory of the Leisure Class* (1899; rpt. New York: Mentor, 1953), p. 126.

29. Ibid., p. 34.

30. Ibid.

31. Hofstadter, *Anti-Intellectualism*, p. 190.

32. Henry James, *The Bostonians* (1886; rpt. New York: Modern Library, 1965), p. 343. Subsequent references are to this edition; page numbers will be provided in the text.

33. Wasserstrom, *Heiress*, p. 34.

34. Hofstadter, *American Political Tradition*, p. 164.

35. Veblen, *Theory of the Leisure Class*, p. 70.

36. Wiebe, *Search for Order*, pp. 2-3.

37. Erik H. Erikson, *Childhood and Society*, 2d ed. (1950; rpt. New York: W. W. Norton, 1963), p. 323.

38. Ibid.

39. Hofstadter, *American Political Tradition*, p. 165.

40. Ibid., p. 167.

41. Richard Hofstadter, *Social Darwinism in American Thought*, rev. ed. (Boston: Beacon Press, 1955), p. 31.

42. Higham, "From Boundlessness to Consolidation," p. 4.

43. Wiebe, *Search for Order*, pp. 11-12.

44. Higham, "From Boundlessness to Consolidation," p. 5.

45. Hofstadter, *Social Darwinism*, p. 35.

46. Veblen, *Theory of the Leisure Class*, p. 170.

47. Ibid., p. 171.

48. Ibid., p. 175.

49. C. R. Henderson, "Business Men and Social Theorists," *American Journal of Sociology*, 1 (1896), 385-86.

50. Hofstadter, *Social Darwinism*, p. 201.

51. Cochran and Miller, *Social History*, p. 119.

52. Cited in Hofstadter, *American Political Tradition*, p. 168.

53. It can, however, be argued with considerable weight that at least some of these tactics, while deplorable, were a necessary stage in the socioeconomic development experienced by all industrialized nations. This stage eventually led to a positive one including better working conditions and tougher laws concerning business ethics. It is notable in this regard that huge corporations, for all their disadvantages and excesses, were among the first businesses to permit unionization, while smaller, independent operations were the last holdouts against the labor movement.

54. Wasserstrom, *Heiress*, p. 35.

55. Michael Paul Rogin, *Fathers and Children* (New York: Alfred A. Knopf, 1975), p. 79.

56. Diamond, *In Search of the Primitive*, p. 144.

57. Rogin, *Fathers and Children*, p. 6.

58. Winthrop D. Jordan, *White over Black* (Baltimore: Penguin Books, 1969), pp. 90-91.

59. Cited in Rogin, *Fathers and Children*, p. 11.

60. See Leslie A. Fiedler, *The Return of the Vanishing American* (1968; rpt. New York: Stein and Day, 1969), pp. 169-87.

61. Rogin, *Fathers and Children*, p. 125.

62. Leo Marx, *The Machine in the Garden* (New York: Oxford Univ. Press, 1964), p. 69.

63. Cited in Matthew Josephson, *The Robber Barons* (1934; rpt. New York: Harcourt, Brace and World, 1962), p. 98.

64. Ibid., pp. 81-82.

65. Cited in ibid., p. 229.

66. Ibid., p. 266.

67. Cited in ibid., p. 151.

68. Thomas C. Cochran, "The Legend of the Robber Barons," *The Pennsylvania Magazine of History and Biography*, 74, no. 3 (July 1950), 309.

69. Ibid.

70. Veblen, "Captain of Industry," p. 108.

71. Erikson, *Childhood and Society*, p. 321.

72. Marx, *Machine in the Garden*, p. 29.

73. Veblen, *Theory of the Leisure Class*, p. 38.

74. See Erikson, *Childhood and Society*, p. 321.

75. Henry Adams, *The Education of Henry Adams* (1906; rpt. Boston: Houghton Mifflin, 1961), p. 382.

76. Ibid., pp. 383-84.

77. Marx, *Machine in the Garden*, p. 349.

78. Cited in ibid., p. 208.

CHAPTER 4. HE-MAN MAGAZINES AND THE AMERICAN SUPER-MALE

1. Richard Slotkin, *Regeneration through Violence* (Middletown, Conn.: Wesleyan Univ. Press, 1973), p. 564.

2. Ibid.

3. John G. Cawelti, *The Six-Gun Mystique* (Bowling Green, Ohio: Bowling Green Univ. Popular Press, 1969), pp. 10-11.

4. Ibid., p. 14.

5. Ibid., pp. 14-15.

6. Thorstein Veblen, *The Theory of the Leisure Class* (1899; rpt. New York: Mentor, 1953), p. 170.

7. Ibid., p. 70.

8. Cited in Edward G. White, *The Eastern Establishment and the Western Experience* (New Haven, Conn.: Yale Univ. Press, 1968), p. 91.

9. Ibid., p. 93.

10. Cawelti, *Six-Gun Mystique*, p. 73.

11. See Erik Erikson, *Childhood and Society*, 2d ed. (1950; rpt. New York: W. W. Norton, 1963), p. 291.

12. Ibid.

13. *True*, January 1975, p. 21.

14. Harry Egner, "Argo-Notes from the Publisher," *Argosy*, November 1974, p. 6.

15. F. Scott Fitzgerald, *The Last Tycoon* (New York: Charles Scribner's Sons, 1941), p. 163.

16. Slotkin, *Regeneration through Violence*, p. 557.

17. Ibid.

18. Veblen, *Theory of the Leisure Class*, pp. 171, 175.

19. Walter Van Tilburg Clark, "Buck in the Hills," *Climax*, December 1961, p. 73.

20. Henry Nash Smith, *Virgin Land* (Cambridge: Harvard Univ. Press, 1950), p. 89. Charles Averill wrote the novel *Kit Carson, The Prince of the Gold Hunters; or the Adventures of the Sacramento* in 1849.

21. Matthew Josephson, *The Robber Barons* (1934; rpt. New York: Harcourt, Brace and World, 1962), p. 335.

22. Slotkin, *Regeneration through Violence*, pp. 564-65.

23. Bert Randolph Sugar, "The Cowboy Hall of Fame," *Argosy*, November 1974, p. 44.

24. Smith, *Virgin Land*, p. 100.

25. Ibid., p. 107.

26. Slotkin, *Regeneration through Violence*, pp. 556-57.

27. Will E. Price, "Stranger in Town," *Climax*, October 1957, pp. 23-24.

28. Cawelti, *Six-Gun Mystique*, p. 58.

29. John Blake, "Tarzan of the Tetons," *Climax*, October 1957, p. 12.

30. Ibid.

31. Ibid.

32. Ibid., p. 15.

33. Sigmund Freud, *Civilization and Its Discontents*, ed. James Strachey (1930; rpt. New York: W. W. Norton, 1961), p. 27.

34. Ibid., p. 33.

35. Slotkin, *Regeneration through Violence*, p. 556.

36. Freud, *Civilization*, p. 43.

37. Jim Scott, "The Vigilantes Are Back!" *Argosy*, February 1975, p. 30.

38. Ibid., p. 32.

39. Emile C. Schurmacher, "The Secret Mission of Marcus Whitman," *Stag*, October 1956, p. 17.

40. Smith, *Virgin Land*, pp. 54-55.

41. Len Guttridge, "The Flying Fool," *Stag*, December 1964, p. 16.

42. Josh Matlock, "Bless You, Damn You...Love, Dad," *True*, November 1974, p. 62.

43. Ibid.

44. William Hartley and Ellen Hartley, "Booze and Babes at Canaveral," *Climax*, December 1961, p. 16.

45. Bernard Fall, "The French Take It with Them," *Climax*, December 1961, p. 35.

46. Horace Phillips, "White Slave of Melville Island," *Stag*, October 1956, p. 35.

47. Ron Bishop, "The Big Squeal," *True*, January 1975, p. 24.

48. Ibid., p. 26.

49. Cited in R. Brent Bonah and Sheila Shively, *The Language Lens* (Englewood Cliffs, N.J.: Prentice-Hall, 1974), pp. 173-74.

50. Bishop, "Big Squeal," p. 28.

51. Robert Pirsig, "Come Ride with Me," *True*, July 1974, p. 21.

52. Randy Neuman, "Motocross: Hills, Dales, Bumps and Mud," *Argosy*, April 1975, p. 60. The idea here concerning the sexual properties of the machine recalls James Dickey's poem "Cherrylog Road" in which a young couple copulates in the back seat of a wrecked automobile before departing, she along Cherrylog Road, he on a motorcycle, ". . . a bicycle fleshed / With power."

53. Cited in Marx, *Machine in the Garden*, p. 208.

54. Pat Graves, "Polo with 4-Wheel Ponies," *True*, July 1966, p. 52.

55. Bishop, "Big Squeal," p. 26.

56. *True*, January 1975, p. 21.

SELECTED BIBLIOGRAPHY

Acton, William. *The Functions and Disorders of the Reproductive Organs in Childhood, Youth, Adult Age, and Advanced Life Considered in Their Physiological, Social, and Moral Relations.* 3d Amer. ed. Philadelphia: n.p., 1871.

Adams, Henry. *The Education of Henry Adams.* 1906. Reprint. Boston: Houghton Mifflin, 1961.

Baker, Elizabeth F. *Technology and Woman's Work.* New York: Columbia Univ. Press, 1964.

Barker-Benfield, G. J. *The Horrors of the Half-Known Life: Male Attitudes toward Women and Sexuality in Nineteenth-Century America.* New York: Harper and Row, 1976.

Beecher, Catharine. *The Elements of Mental and Moral Philosophy, Founded upon Experience, Reason and the Bible.* Hartford, Conn.: n.p., 1831.

——. *An Essay on the Education of Female Teachers.* New York: Van Nostrand and Dwight, 1835.

——. *Suggestions Respecting Improvements in Education, Presented to the Trustees.* Hartford, Conn.: Packard and Butler, 1829.

Beecher, Catharine E., and Harriet Beecher Stowe. *The American Woman's Home: Or, Principles of Domestic Science; Being a Guide to the Formation and Maintenance of Economical, Healthful, Beautiful, and Christian Homes.* New York: J. B. Ford, 1869.

Bishop, Ron. "The Big Squeal." *True,* January 1975.

Blake, John. "Tarzan of the Tetons." *Climax,* October 1957.

Blau, Joseph L., ed. *Social Theories of Jacksonian Democracy: Representative Writings of the Period, 1825-1850*. New York: Liberal Arts Press, 1947.

Bonah, R. Brent, and Sheila Shively. *The Language Lens*. Englewood Cliffs, N.J.: Prentice-Hall, 1974.

Branch, E. Douglas. *The Sentimental Years: 1836-1860*. New York: Hill and Wang, 1934.

Brooks, William K. "The Condition of Women from a Zoological Point of View." *Popular Science Monthly*, 15 (1879), 145-55.

Brown, Herbert Ross. *The Sentimental Novel in America: 1789-1860*. Durham, N.C.: Duke Univ. Press, 1940.

Bunyan, John. *The Pilgrim's Progress*. 1677. Reprint. New York: James Pott and Co., n.d.

Cawelti, John G. *The Six-Gun Mystique*. Bowling Green, Ohio: Bowling Green Univ. Popular Press, 1969.

Cianfrani, Theodore. *A Short History of Obstetrics and Gynecology*. Springfield, Mass.: Charles C. Thomas, 1960.

Claiborne, Nathaniel H. *Notes on the War in the South*. Richmond, Va.: n.p., 1819.

Clark, Walter Van Tilburg. "Buck in the Hills." *Climax*, December 1961.

Clemens, Samuel Langhorne (Mark Twain). *Adventures of Huckleberry Finn*. Edited by Sculley Bradley, Richmond Croom Beatty, and E. Hudson Long. 1885. Reprint. New York: W. W. Norton, 1961.

Clouston, T. S. *Female Education from a Medical Point of View*. Edinburgh: n.p., 1882.

Cochran, Thomas C. 'The Legend of the Robber Barons." *The Pennsylvania Magazine of History and Biography*, 74, no. 3 (July 1950), 307-21.

Cochran, Thomas C., and William Miller. *A Social History of Industrial America*. Rev. ed. New York: Harper and Brothers, 1961.

Congressional Record. 49th Congress, 1st Session, 26 March 1886.

Conkling, Alfred R. *Life and Letters of Roscoe Conkling*. New York: n.p., 1889.

Cooper, James Fenimore. *Notions of the Americans*. Vol. I, London: n.p., 1828; Vol. II, Philadelphia: n.p., 1836.

———. *Home as Found*. 1838. Reprint. New York: Capricorn, 1961.

Dana, Richard Henry. *Two Years before the Mast: A Personal Narrative*. 1840. Reprint. New York: Signet, 1964.

Degler, Carl N. *Out of Our Past: The Forces That Shaped Modern America*. Rev. ed., 1959. Reprint. New York: Harper and Row, 1970.

———. "What Ought to Be and What Was: Woman's Sexuality in the Nineteenth Century." *American Historical Review*, 70 (December 1974), 1467-90.

Demos, John. "The American Family in Past Time." *The American Scholar*, 43 (Summer 1974), 422-46.

Diamond, Sigmund. *The Reputation of the American Businessman*. Cambridge: Harvard Univ. Press, 1955.

Diamond, Stanley. *In Search of the Primitive: A Critique of Civilization*. New Brunswick, N.J.: Transaction Books, 1974.

Douglas, Ann. *The Feminization of American Culture*. New York: Knopf, 1977.

Duberman, Martin. Review of *The Horrors of the Half-Known Life: Male Attitudes toward Women and Sexuality in Nineteenth-Century America*, by G. J. Barker-Benfield. *The New York Times Book Review*, 18 January 1976, pp. 4, 15.

Duffey, Eliza B. *The Relations of the Sexes*. New York: n.p., 1876.

Editorial. *Nation*, 10 (9 June 1870), 367.

Editorial. *The New York Times*, 8 October 1834.

Editorial. *Richmond Enquirer*, 3 January 1828.

Egner, Harry. "Argo-Notes from the Publisher."*Argosy*, November 1974, p. 6.

Elkins, Stanley M. *Slavery: A Problem in American Institutional and Intellectual Life*. 2d ed. Chicago: Univ. of Chicago Press, 1968.

Erikson, Erik H. *Childhood and Society*. 2d ed. New York: W. W. Norton, 1963.

Fall, Bernard. "The French Take It with Them." *Climax*, December 1961.

Fiedler, Leslie A. *Cross the Border—Close the Gap*. New York: Stein and Day, 1972.

———. *Love and Death in the American Novel*. 2d ed. New York: Stein and Day, 1966.

——— *No! In Thunder: Essays on Myth and Literature*. 2d ed. New York: Stein and Day, 1972.

———. *The Return of the Vanishing American*. 1968. Reprint. New York: Stein and Day, 1969.

———. *Waiting for the End*. New York: Stein and Day, 1964.

Filene, Peter Gabriel. *Him/Her/Self: Sex Roles in Modern America*. New York: New American Library, 1974.

Fitzgerald, F. Scott. *The Last Tycoon*. New York: Charles Scribner's Sons, 1941.

Fox-Genovese, Elizabeth. "Psychohistory versus Psychodeterminism: The Case of Rogin's Jackson."*Reviews in American History*, 3 (December 1975), 407-18.

Frederic, Harold. *The Damnation of Theron Ware*. 1896. Reprint. New York: Holt, Rinehart and Winston, 1960.

Freud, Sigmund. *Civilization and Its Discontents*. Edited by James Strachey. 1930. Reprint. New York: W. W. Norton, 1961.

Friedman, Lawrence J. *Inventors of the Promised Land*. New York: Alfred A. Knopf, 1975.

Galbraith, John Kenneth. *American Capitalism: The Concept of Countervailing Power*. 1952. Reprint. Boston: Houghton Mifflin, 1962.

Gardner, Augustus Kinsley. *History of the Art of Mid-wifery*. New York: Stringer and Townshend, 1852.

Goetzmann, William H. "The Mountain Man as Jacksonian Man." In *The American Culture: Approaches to the Study of the United States*, edited by Hennig Cohen. Boston: Houghton Mifflin, 1968.

Gorer, Geoffrey. *The American People: A Study in National Character*. Rev. ed. New York: W. W. Norton, 1964.

Graves, Pat. "Polo with 4-Wheel Ponies." *True*, July 1966.

Graham, Sylvester. *Chastity, In a Course of Lectures to Young Men; Intended also, for the Serious Consideration of Parents and Guardians*. New York: Fowler and Wells, n.d.

Guttridge, Len. "The Flying Fool." *Stag*, December 1964.

Hale, Nathan G. *Freud and the Americans: The Beginning of Psychoanalysis in the United States, 1876-1917*. New York: Oxford Univ. Press, 1971.

Hale, Sarah Josepha. *Sketches of American Character*. Boston: n.p., 1838.

Hall, G. Stanley, *Adolescence: Its Psychology and Its Relations to Physiology, Anthropology, Sociology, Sex, Crime, Religion and Education*. 2 vols. New York: Appleton, 1904.

Haller, John S., and Robin M. Haller. *The Physician and Sexuality in Victorian America*. Urbana: Univ. of Illinois Press, 1974.

Hardaker, M. A. "Science and the Woman Question." *Popular Science Monthly*, 20 (1882), 577-84.

Harris, Seale. *Woman's Surgeon*. New York: Macmillan, 1950.

Hartley, William and Ellen Hartley. "Booze and Babes at Canaveral." *Climax*, December 1961.

Hawthorne, Nathaniel. *The Blithedale Romance*. 1852. Reprint. New York: W. W. Norton, 1958.

———. *The Scarlet Letter*. Edited by Sculley Bradley, Richmond Croom Beatty, and E. Hudson Long. 1850. Reprint. New York: W. W. Norton, 1961.

Henderson, C. R. "Business Men and Social Theorists." *American Journal of Sociology*, 1 (1896), 385-97.

Higham, John. "From Boundlessness to Consolidation: The Transformation of American Culture, 1848-1860." William L. Clements Library. 1969. Reprinted in *The Bobbs-Merrill Reprint Series in American History*, No. H-414.

Hofstadter, Richard. *The American Political Tradition and the Men Who Made It*. New York: Vintage, 1948.

————. *Anti-Intellectualism in American Life*. New York: Vintage, 1962.

————. *Social Darwinism in American Thought*. Rev. ed. Boston: Beacon Press, 1955.

Holbrook, M. L. *Parturition without Pain: A Code of Directions for Escaping from the Primal Curse*. New York: n.p., 1882.

Holley, O. L. *The Connexion between the Mechanic Arts and the Welfare of the States: An Address Delivered before the Mechanics of Troy, at Their Request on the 4th of July, 1825*. Troy, N.Y.: n.p., 1825.

Irving, Washington. "Rip Van Winkle." 1819. Reprinted in *Washington Irving: Selected Prose*, edited by Stanley T. Williams, pp. 90-107. New York: Holt, Rinehart and Winston, 1950.

Jackson, Andrew. *Correspondence of Andrew Jackson*. Edited by John Spencer Bassett. Vol. III. Washington, D.C.: n.p., 1928.

James, Henry. *The Bostonians*. 1886. Reprint. New York: Modern Library, 1965.

Jordon, Winthrop D. *White over Black: American Attitudes toward the Negro, 1550-1812*. Baltimore: Penguin Books, 1969.

Josephson, Matthew. *The Robber Barons: The Great American Capitalists, 1861-1901*. 1934. Reprint. New York: Harcourt, Brace and World, 1962.

Kellogg, J. H. *Plain Facts for Both Sexes*. 1879. Reprint. Battle Creek, Mich.: Good Health Publishing Co., 1910.

Kennedy, David M. *Birth Control in America: The Career of Margaret Sanger*. New Haven, Conn.: Yale Univ. Press, 1970.

Lawrence, D. H. *Studies in Classical American Literature*. 1923. Reprint. New York: Viking, 1964.

Lerner, Gerda. "The Lady and the Mill Girl: Changes in the Status of Women in the Age of Jackson." *Mid-Continent American Studies Journal*, 10 (Spring 1969), 5-15.

Lewis, R.W.B. *The American Adam: Innocence, Tragedy, and Tradition in the Nineteenth Century*. Chicago: Univ. of Chicago Press, 1955.

McClung, John A. *Sketches of Western Adventure*. Maysville, Ky.: n.p., 1832.

Marx, Leo. *The Machine in the Garden: Technology and the Pastoral Ideal in America*. New York: Oxford Univ. Press, 1964.

Matlock, Josh. "Bless You, Damn You...Love, Dad: The Confessions of an American Father." *True*, November 1974.

Mead, Margaret. *Male and Female: A Study of the Sexes in a Changing World*. 1950. Reprint. Harmondsworth, Middlesex, England: Pelican Books, 1962.

Meigs, Charles D. *Lecture on Some of the Distinctive Characteristics of the Female. Delivered before the Class of the Jefferson Medical College, January 5, 1847*. Philadelphia: n.p., 1847.

Melville, Herman. *Moby-Dick*. Edited by Harrison Hayford and Hershel Parker. 1851. Reprint. New York: W. W. Norton, 1967.

Meyer, Donald B. *The Positive Thinkers*. Garden City, N.Y.: Doubleday, 1965.

Meyers, Marvin. *The Jacksonian Persuasion: Politics and Belief*. 2d ed. Stanford, Calif.: Stanford Univ. Press, 1960.

Mitchell, S. Weir. *Doctor and Patient*. Philadelphia: J. B. Lippincott, 1887.

Neuman, Randy. "Motocross: Hills, Dales, Bumps and Mud." *Argosy*, April 1975.

Pessen, Edward. *Jacksonian America: Society, Personality, and Politics*. Homewood, Ill.: Dorsey Press, 1969.

Phillips, Horace. "White Slave of Melville Island." *Stag*, October 1956.

Pierson, George Wilson. *Tocqueville and Beaumont in America*. New York: Oxford Univ. Press, 1938.

Pirsig, Robert. "Come Ride with Me." *True*, July 1974.

Pivar, David J. *Purity Crusade: Sexual Morality and Social Control, 1868-1900*. Westport, Conn.: Greenwood Press, 1973.

Platt, Thomas Collier. *Autobiography*. New York: n.p., 1910.

Price, Will E. "Stranger in Town."*Climax*, October 1957.

Richardson, James D., ed. *Messages and Papers of the Presidents, 1789-1897*. Vols. II and III. Washington, D.C.: n.p., 1896.

Rieff, Philip. *Freud: The Mind of the Moralist*. Garden City, N.Y.: Doubleday-Anchor, 1959.

Riesman, David, et al. *The Lonely Crowd: A Study of the Changing American Character*. New Haven, Conn.: Yale Univ. Press, 1950.

Rogin, Michael Paul. *Fathers and Children: Andrew Jackson and the Subjugation of the American Indian*. New York: Alfred A. Knopf, 1975.

Rostow, W. W. *The Stages of Economic Growth, A Non-Communist Manifesto*. Cambridge: Harvard Univ. Press, 1960.

Rourke, Constance. *The Roots of American Culture*. New York: Harcourt, Brace and Co., 1942.

Santayana, George. *Character and Opinion in the United States*. 1920. Reprint. New York: Charles Scribner's Sons, 1921.

Saveth, Edward N. "The Problem of American Family History." *American Quarterly*, 21 (Summer 1969), 311-29.

Schlesinger, Arthur M. *The Age of Jackson*. Boston: Little, Brown, 1945.

Schurmacher, Emile. "The Secret Mission of Marcus Whitman." *Stag*, October 1956.

Scott, Jim. "The Vigilantes Are Back!" *Argosy*, February 1975.

Sklar, Kathryn Kish. *Catharine Beecher: A Study in American Domesticity*. New Haven, Conn.: Yale Univ. Press, 1973.

Slotkin, Richard. *Regeneration through Violence: The Mythology of the Amer-*

ican Frontier, 1600-1860. Middletown, Conn.: Wesleyan Univ. Press, 1973.

Smith, A. L. "Higher Education of Women and Race Suicide." *Popular Science Monthly,* 66 (1905), 466-73.

Smith, Daniel Scott. "Child-Naming Patterns and Family Structure Change: Hingham, Massachusetts, 1640-1880." Paper prepared for the Clark University Conference on the Famiy and Social Structure, 27-29 April 1972.

Smith, Henry Nash. *Virgin Land: The American West as Symbol and Myth.* Cambridge: Harvard Univ. Press, 1950.

Smith-Rosenberg, Carroll. "The Hysterical Woman: Sex Roles and Role Conflict in 19th-Century America." *Social Research,* 39 (Winter 1972), 652-78.

Smith-Rosenberg, Carroll, and Charles Rosenberg. "The Female Animal: Medical and Biological Views of Woman and Her Role in Nineteenth-Century America." *The Journal of American History,* 60 (September 1973), 332-56.

Spencer, Herbert. *The Study of Sociology.* New York: n.p., 1896.

Sugar, Bert Randolph. "The Cowboy Hall of Fame." *Argosy,* November 1974.

Talbot, George F. "The Political Rights and Duties of Women." *Popular Science Monthly,* 49 (1896), 80-97.

Taylor, George Rogers. *The Transportation Revolution.* New York: Harper and Row, 1968.

Taylor, William R. *Cavalier and Yankee: The Old South and American National Character.* New York: George Braziller, 1961.

The Tennessee Farmer; or, Farmer Jackson in New York. Pamphlet by an anonymous author, n.p., n.d.

Thoreau, Henry David. *Walden and Civil Disobedience.* Edited by Owen Thomas. 1854. Reprint. New York: W. W. Norton, 1966.

Tocqueville, Alexis de. *Democracy in America.* 2 vols. Translated by Henry Reeves. 1850. Reprint. New York: A. S. Barnes, 1858.

Topinard, Paul. *Anthropology.* London: n.p., 1878.

Trecker, Janice Law. "Sex, Science and Education." *American Quarterly,* 26 (October 1974), 352-66.

True, January 1975.

Veblen, Thorstein. "The Captain of Industry." *Absentee Ownership and Business Enterprise in Recent Times: The Case of America.* 1923. Reprinted in *Democracy and the Gospel of Wealth,* edited by Gail Kennedy, pp. 102-11. Boston: D. C. Heath, 1949.

———. *The Theory of the Leisure Class: An Economic Study of Institutions.* 1899. Reprint. New York: Mentor, 1953.

Waldo, Samuel Putnam. *Memoirs of Andrew Jackson*. 3d ed. Hartford, Conn.: n.p., 1819.

Walters, Ronald G., ed. *Primers for Prudery: Sexual Advice to Victorian America*. Englewood Cliffs, N.J.: Prentice-Hall, 1974.

Ward, John William. *Andrew Jackson: Symbol for an Age*. New York: Oxford Univ. Press, 1962.

Wasserstrom, William. *Heiress of All the Ages: Sex and Sentiment in the Genteel Tradition*. Minneapolis: Univ. of Minnesota Press, 1959.

Welter, Barbara. "The Cult of True Womanhood: 1820-1860." *American Quarterly*, 18 (Summer 1966), 151-74.

White, Edward G. *The Eastern Establishment and the Western Experience*. New Haven, Conn.: Yale Univ. Press, 1968.

Wiebe, Robert H. *The Search for Order, 1877-1920*. New York: Hill and Wang, 1967.

Wyatt-Brown, Bertram. "The Abolitionist Controversy: Men of Blood, Men of God." In *Men, Women, and Issues in American History*, edited by Howard H. Quint and Milton Cantor, vol. I, pp. 215-33. Homewood, Ill.: Dorsey Press, 1975.

Wylie, Philip. *Generation of Vipers*. New York: Rinehart, 1942.

Young, Philip. "Fallen from Time: The Mythic Rip Van Winkle." In *Psychoanalysis and American Fiction*, edited by Irving Malin, pp. 23-45. New York: E. P. Dutton, 1965.

INDEX

About the Author

DAVID G. PUGH has been a Visiting Assistant Professor of English at Willamette University, Salem, Oregon, and at Oregon State University, Corvallis. He is currently a Writing/Research Consultant for Shipley Associates, Bountiful, Utah. His articles have been published in the *Journal of American Culture*, *Illinois Quarterly*, and *The Markham Review*.

audacity - risk (20), take a gamble